STARTUPS
and Downs

THE SECRETS OF RESILIENT ENTREPRENEURS

STARTUPS
and Downs

MONA BIJOOR

Copyright © 2019 **Mona Bijoor**

Indigo River Publishing
3 West Garden Street, Ste. 352
Pensacola, FL 32502
www.indigoriverpublishing.com

Editors: Dianna Gravemann, Joey Bartolomeo, and Regina Cornell
Cover & Book Design: mycustombookcover.com

Ordering Information:
Quantity sales: Special discounts are available on quantity purchases by corporations, associations, and others. For details, contact the publisher at the address above.

Orders by US trade bookstores and wholesalers: Please contact the publisher at the address above.

Printed in the United States of America

Library of Congress Control Number: 2019946198

ISBN: Paperback: 978-1-950906-08-6 (paperback), 978-1-950906-09-3 (ebook)

First Edition

With Indigo River Publishing, you can always expect great books, strong voices, and mean-ingful messages. Most importantly, you'll always find . . . words worth reading.

For Jaya and Yana, the next generation of entrepreneurs

Contents

INTRODUCTION

Ten years ago, I was a first-time founder, using my own capital to fund my own idea: to start a software business in the fashion industry. I felt pressure to grow rapidly (otherwise I thought I'd be wasting time and money), so I didn't take time to surround myself with a sound group of mentors who could help navigate the ups and downs of building a business. I also didn't have the luxury of a professional coach, a therapist, or anyone besides my family to help me deal with the stress. I thought that with enough passion and persistence I could be successful on my own and figure out the unknowns along the way.

I'm proud to say that my company, JOOR, took off. With seven offices globally, serving thousands of brands and retailers and processing billions of dollars of orders, our software changed the way the entire fashion industry works and spawned a lot of competition. It wasn't easy to get to that place. I weathered the hardship of raising over $20 million in capital, hiring a team and then losing some of them, creating a product and then fending off competition, and building a brand and then ultimately leaving the company to start a new business in a new industry. The whole process was hard and painful, and there were many days when it was difficult to find the strength to keep going. Being a founder was probably the most challenging thing I've done in my life—with the exception of giving birth to my children, which, by the way, was harder!

The thing is, building a company didn't need to be that difficult. Many of the issues that I found challenging (for example, hiring and firing) were actually just in my head.

I've spent the past couple of years advising hundreds of first-time founders, and my conversations with them were the inspiration for this book. I came to realize that there is a set of issues that all business owners face at one time or another. But these common challenges—pitching investors, losing key employees, dealing with the competition—aren't something people automatically know how to deal with from the get-go. Most founders have had the same thoughts I had when I first began: we all believe we can use our wits and work ethic to overcome any issue we encounter.

I kept wondering: If these issues are so common, why don't people get the answers they need the most? Is it because first-time founders are too busy to seek them? Do their egos compel them to come up with solutions by themselves? Then it dawned on me: The root of the problem is that many entrepreneurs simply don't frame their problems in a way that makes them manageable. Problems either get ignored or blown out of proportion, or they completely derail the founder.

In this book, I will share with you what I think all business owners (big, small, start-up, or established) need to know about overcoming the challenges every entrepreneur experiences during his or her journey. But I also want you to learn how having the right mind-set—one that is purpose-driven and based on seven simple principles—is the real key to navigating obstacles and bouncing back quickly from whatever life throws at you. Hands down, these principles are the one thing that people who persevere and succeed have in common. That's why, in addition to my own story, this book is full of interviews with noteworthy founders who often shifted their ways of thinking in order to grow their businesses quickly and profitably. My hope is that our stories will inspire you to find your true purpose and achieve success too.

ONE

THE MIND-SET OF AN ENTREPRENEUR

Both my parents were entrepreneurs. My mom ran a commercial printing business, and my dad owned an executive search firm. And both believed they were in the business of serving customers and making them happy. Sitting around the dinner table, my parents would talk about what happened at work that day. My mom would share stories about a happy couple thrilled with their engraved wedding invitations or talk about a dissatisfied customer who wasn't happy with a typo on his sales flyers. My dad would talk about how he convinced someone to move to Detroit to take a great new job or how he failed to find the right candidate for a client but still kept trying. Stories about pleasing customers (and going above and beyond what was expected) would often be our daily dinner conversation.

It gave me a sense of pride that my parents—both in very different businesses—were always on the customer's side. When unhappy customers would appear, they would always redo the work and reimburse, waive, or forgo payment just to make their customers happy. It felt like something more holy than pleasing clients or displaying generosity; to me, it felt like true service. Even when they were fully in the right and the client was wrong, they would still take the customer's side.

And it was this service that drove them. Rather than feeling exhausted by their customers, they always seemed teeming with energy. At one point, my dad worked full-time while getting his MBA at night and still did the accounting for my mom's business. I would often ask them why they worked so much. They would tell me that giving up wasn't an option for them. They believed they could make their businesses successful no matter the obstacle. I would ask them whether they were worried about failing. They would look at me and say, "We are completely customer-focused. Our customers can depend on us to make them happy. If they are happy, then they will always return to us. We can't really fail, because our motivation is to always be helpful to our customers, employees, and the community around us." They had defined what success meant to them: success was running a profitable business in which customers were truly satisfied with the services they received. They taught me that anything was possible when you define success and find your *why*, the thing that truly motivates you. More importantly, I learned that when you put in the work, you must always trust the process and not get impatient waiting for a successful outcome.

Ironically, though, when I applied to colleges, my parents encouraged me to pursue science, math, or anything BUT business. They knew, down to their bones, that owning a business was hard and required a whole lot of sacrifice.

After I graduated from college with a degree in human biology, I did what most pre-professional University of Pennsylvania kids did: I got a job in management consulting. I loved serving clients, but I knew that executing the advice was way more fun than providing advice. After completing my MBA, I started working as a strategist at a fashion luxury house (to get in the door) and then as a fashion buyer with full profit-and-loss responsibility.

As a buyer, I worked at a large retailer where the leadership couldn't stop discounting their product. Rather than finding the courage to design product that suited the needs of their clients, they ran promotion after promotion, devaluing the brand. I learned firsthand that a successful business is never about price. It's always about having the best product or service that truly fulfills the pain point of the customer you serve.

As I watched the retailer's brand equity erode day by day, I knew I couldn't work for someone else. I wanted to set my own strategic direction, build a product that solved a true pain point, and make my own mistakes rather than someone else's. I set out to find a true problem I could solve. Leveraging my knowledge of the fashion space, I found a void in the market: The commerce between fashion brands and retailers was completely offline, and there was no online backbone to the industry. There needed to be a platform where brands and retailers could discover, connect, and transact online.

When I launched my business, I used my parents' experience as a model for how I would launch my own. I cared deeply about the clients we served. Customer service became the underpinning of my business. It was not just about offering a stellar product; it was also about offering superior service.

I enjoyed analyzing my parents' approach to building their businesses. On paper, it's often easy to figure out why some businesses work and some don't, but there's always a lot more to it. So, as I was writing this book, I decided to interview other successful entrepreneurs so that I could get inside their heads and understand the mentalities that drove their success. It didn't matter whether I was talking to founders who worked in finance, health care, or beauty; or whether they were self-made or they were billionaires—these seven tenets came up time and time again:

1. **Everything is possible.**

This is the kid-like belief that the sky's the limit. There is no past experience or humiliating failure that stops these entrepreneurs from believing that anything is possible. Unfulfilled dreams or constantly being told no does not hold them back. Expectations aren't lowered because of their past failures or mistakes. Many of us get caught up in "How can I do it? I don't have money, time, or resources," and that thinking stops us from trying. But these entrepreneurs set their intention and start taking action. Their momentum ultimately leads them to success and realizing their vision.

2. **Failure is not an option.**

This credo is a trickier one because failure happens to many successful entrepreneurs. It's just the way these founders view failure that differs from those who give up. Successful entrepreneurs view failure as simply an outcome they don't want to see more of. Success is viewed as an outcome they do want and a signal that they should do more of whatever got them there. It's black or white—and nonemotional. If these entrepreneurs don't like the outcome, then it's simply viewed as a trigger to change the tactic and create, hopefully, a positive result. This philosophy is summarized well in Henry Ford's quote: "Failure is simply the opportunity to begin again, this time more intelligently."

3. Realism and optimism are friends.

There are two ways to be optimistic: realistically and unrealistically. Unrealistic optimists believe that good things will happen and don't focus on the responsibility they should take in finding success. Meanwhile, realistic optimists believe they possess the power to make success happen, and to make it happen in spite of any circumstance or small failures along the way.

4. You need to find your *why*.

All of the entrepreneurs I interviewed have a compelling reason to get out of bed in the morning—especially when they don't want to. It is their reason for being and why they give 110 percent to their businesses every day. Many of these entrepreneurs have also established a cost associated with NOT achieving their mission. They believe certain doors will close or they won't have access to certain opportunities if they don't achieve their *why*. And the reason goes beyond their own personal upside. Achieving the result means it will help their broader family, their community, or the world at large.

5. A constant state of flow leads to success.

Flow is a zen-like state where once the vision and the direction are set, then action will flow. But sometimes the actions taken don't turn out the way the entrepreneurs had expected. This is when "going with the flow" takes over. Entrepreneurs who hold this belief stay open to the possibilities of unexpected outcomes that can ultimately lead them to a better place. Entrepreneurs aren't wedded to HOW things are going to happen. They are wedded to WHY they want to head in a certain direction.

6.   The answers lie within.

Many of us are caught up with defining success by how others have achieved it. The entrepreneurs I spoke with have their own definitions of success. They've long ago stopped comparing their lives to others'. Only we have the power to change our perceptions of success. Once we stop looking on the outside and turn within, then we can find contentment.

7.   You must trust the process.

People have a timeline of success in their heads. They form this timeline early in life, and when things don't go according to that timeline, disappointment happens. "I will be married by twenty-five," "I will make my first million at thirty," "I will sell my company at thirty-five," and on and on. We are caught up in a world of instant gratification. Nothing comes fast enough—not our Uber, not our dinner, not our paycheck. Trusting the process, for these entrepreneurs, means waking up every day and taking massive action without a set timeline in mind, because they believe that a lot of small wins translate into big successes—and big success doesn't come in an instant.

The entrepreneurs you'll meet in this book consider these tenets proven facts, and they're embedded in their psyches. Yet this made me wonder: If you *haven't* had experiences that prove these principles to yourself, then how do you get in the mind-set of a successful entrepreneur? The answer is simple: take big, bold actions (run a marathon or start a side hustle) and set out to prove the principles to yourself as often as you can. If you can unlock these beliefs and internalize them as truths, then you can achieve anything.

Before I start filling you in on all of the other secrets, tools, and nitty-gritty details that you need to launch a money-making enterprise, there's one thing I want you to know: the difference between success and failure is your mind-set. It might sound a little woo-woo, but I've discovered that many successful entrepreneurs—even the badass bosses—share a certain type of spirituality: the ability to find strength and purpose from within that helps them push forward when the road to riches gets challenging.

Inside Story
Interview with Jody Levy, Founder, Chief Executive Officer, and Creative Director of World Waters, maker of WTRMLN WTR

Someone who truly embodies the entrepreneurial mind-set is Jody Levy, the founder of World Waters, a company and brand committed to redefining how and what we drink to nourish our bodies and sustain our ecosystem. Jody's products are sold in over twenty-five thousand stores, including Walmart, Target, and Whole Foods, and she has attracted well-known investors, including Beyoncé and NBA star Chris Paul. World Waters' first product, WTRMLN WTR (watermelon water), was created to solve for the hundreds of millions of pounds of unused watermelons in the United States. These waste melons are either ugly, misshapen, or sunburned, but otherwise perfect from which to press nutrient-dense, hydrating WTRMLN WTR. From Jody I learned how she applies many of the seven principles to grow her business.

1. **What is one transformational experience that impacted your mind-set as an entrepreneur?**

I grew up knowing clearly that my path was one of an artist. When I completed art school at twenty-one, I became a founding member of one of the world's first experience-design firms. Our work was all about bringing together various design disciplines to create immersive stories that explained complex information—for

example, how hydrogen technology is created and sustained—
and making the impossible possible. We invented new software,
hardware, sculpture, and media to tell experiential stories. We
were working with a wide range of clients and businesses, from
Fortune 500 executives to start-up entrepreneurs with wild
dreams. My life as an immersive artist and designer who was
creating never-before-seen events and installations was like boot
camp for developing products, brands, and stories that people
remember and connect with on an emotional level. The process
of defining a core communication (mission) and making sure
every touch-point connects to that story was applied to every one
of my companies and clients. I love this work because it taught
me to believe that nothing is impossible and the world is small;
therefore, you can accomplish everything you want to accomplish.

2. So did doubt ever figure into your process?

There is not much doubt in my mind as it relates to what I can
accomplish. I am a pessimistic optimist—meaning I question
everything and doubt a lot of what people say and do. But, ultimately, I am an eternal optimist. I keep things high energy and
in the realm of possibility: how to solve rather than allow defeat.
I do very much believe that when you are creating something,
you must know the constraints of that operation, solution, team,
and experience. The constraints often define how we come up
with ideas and solutions to a challenge. This idea also flows into
having a solid understanding of what you are not so good at. By
knowing your strengths and weaknesses, you can build a team
to support the end game. Once I understand where I can fit and
best show up to collaborate, everything else becomes [within the]
realm of possibility.

3. **What type of experimentation happened while you were building WTRMLN WTR?**

Every single day of building and running a natural food and beverage company is a process of experimentation. In 2013, when my cofounder shared the fact that there were eight hundred million pounds of unused watermelons because they were aesthetically imperfect (misshapen, sunburned, or discolored, but perfectly nutritious on the inside), I knew there was an opportunity to do something with this food waste. I was inspired to try to create a biofuel—fly rocket ships on watermelon ethanol! But after speaking to an ethanol expert, I soon understood that watermelons aren't as sweet as we think they are, so we couldn't make biofuel. Soon after, we dove into forming World Waters, a company committed to sustainable food production for a healthier world, and we created our first product line: WTRMLN WTR.

4. **When you first started, what were the two or three short-term strategies that you mapped out to achieve your long-term vision?**

When I launched World Waters, the company and our concept of We Grow WTR, we first wanted to determine the most naturally nutritious and hydrating product. We decided to utilize the waste stream of ugly watermelons to create WTRMLN WTR. This was an opportunity to invent not just a product but a lifestyle brand and category simultaneously. I applied—and continue to do so—everything from my work as a strategist and experiential storyteller. We were on the forefront of the clean-food revolution, pushing beyond the natural stores and into mainstream supermarkets. We were offering and educating consumers about electrolytes and hydration, antioxidants, performance-enhancing nutrients that all come naturally from America's superfruit: the watermelon. Everything we have done always aligns with our mission to educate people about the importance of what you put in your body, which directly impacts your wellness and happiness—we call this clean living. For me, success comes down to two things: people want to be happy, and to be happy, they must have their well-being and a sense of purpose. That is where our mission comes from, and why so many amazing, catalytic personalities [professional athletes and celebrities] have invested in our company and helped support our story!

Yet, every step of the way, there were unexpected constraints. Every time someone said, "No, that's not possible," it fueled me to show them it was. It was my eternal optimistic attitude, and my belief in not just *what* we are doing but *how* we are doing it, that has kept me in this flow.

5.   **What runs through your mind when you hit a roadblock, and how do you move forward?**

Building a beverage company is like hitting roadblocks hundreds of times a day. There are so many moments throughout every day that I think, "Why am I doing this?" And then I remind myself that we are building something bigger than ourselves, something that is driven by a powerful and important mission. Clean food is a social justice issue, and we all have the right to have access to clean, affordable food and drinks so that we can live happier and healthier lives. Everyone in our organization is aligned with this mission. It keeps us united and inspired as we get pummeled over and over (as is normal for this crazy industry), gasping for air at the surface.

6. **Was there a setback in your business that tested your resolve?**

When we founded WTRMLN WTR in 2013, my intent was to create the products, build the brand and brand experience, launch it to the world as a platform for love and learning, and hire an industry expert to take over as CEO. It took a handful of years to accomplish, but we did it according to plan. I left to start another project. In September 2016, our CEO had some personal issues and I had to unexpectedly jump back in and take over in the leadership position. This was the single most humbling experience of my life. I'd left when we were doing about $300,000 in topline revenue, and had to jump back in when we had scaled to just under $20 million. There was a complex web that had been woven around our operations, and many hard decisions that had to be undone—deals had to be restructured. It was messy. It was super stressful. But as hard as it was, the experience really refined my ability to lead with love, over-communicate, roll up my sleeves, and be in it with our team to solve problems in unexpected ways.

7. **How do you keep the team motivated during challenging times?**

The natural food and beverage industry is one of the least sexy markets out there. The work has a big mission, but our day-to-day is tactical. The way consumers buy is changing rapidly and making it harder and harder to grow and operate. I find that super-clear over-communication that is grounded in honesty is key. My way of coping with the insanity of an early-stage business is by sharing as much context and information as I can. With my team, there may be a day when I rally them together, tell them what's going on at a corporate level, and say something a little humorous and self-deprecating, like "I'm grumpy and I need to hide out in my office while I deal with this issue." I usually do so with a giant smile on my face and laughing the whole way through—that way, when I bitch and moan about it, everyone knows what's up. Sharing my vulnerabilities gives the team comfort that it's not them and we are all in it together. It also empowers them to help me solve, or to show up for me or for our team in ways they wouldn't know to if I wasn't so open. I do the same with my partners and investors. There is a sanity that becomes clearer even when things aren't clear. I am very focused on full disclosure and transparency with all my partners so that they can show up and be their best selves. I believe business is a team sport and that open communication sets people up to show up as their best self and thrive.

8. **You talk about spirituality in business. What does that mean to you?**

I operate from a place of "spiritual business." I believe that every organization is its own unique organism with its own energetic current. Every part of the whole defines the organism and impacts its wellness and its journey. Every partner, investor, and employee, every person who shares its story and amplifies its purpose, is part of a connected whole.

I believe that money is energy. It is fuel. It is sacred. Like all things in a business, the energy of the money that fuels the organization must be aligned and must flow for progress to continue. I also believe in the concept of what you give, you get back in return. Therefore, when it comes to building and growing businesses, I believe in building mission-driven organizations that give back to communities and society. Your mission is the spirit of your business, and when this purpose is the true north of all decision making, everything aligns to accomplish the goals.

9. How do you manage your spirituality during tough times?

I surround myself with people who stay happy and have a high vibration. I make sure that I spend my time doing the things that I love and that keep me in balance. Sometimes I hack my happiness, meaning I plan the way I spend my time, and what I eat, and how I live, to maximize how I feel. Happiness is about our energetic frequency; it's quantum physics. When I experience stress, I do things to shake it out of my body. I try to dance often. I don't have to talk to anyone on the dance floor; I can get into flow state and shake all the stale energy out of my body. In really intense times, I work hard to rid myself of any fear-based energy (that is typically not my own) and get back to a higher frequency. I do this through biohacking, supplements, clean food, IVs, and energy medicine. I believe in the power of getting into nature and away from the noise and haze of a city. I pull myself out of the hustle and into the woods and take advantage of our innate human ability to be intuitive. I reset, and set myself up to do it all over again.

10. What is the one thing that you think every business owner should believe?

I believe every entrepreneur is different and is in their own hustle and flow for many reasons. For me . . . I believe in Belief. I get really into people who believe in something, and I often see that when a leader comes from that mind-set and heart space, their endeavors thrive. My belief in the journey and the process is strong. As long as I trust my intuition and my decisive choices, I land in the right places. I do not believe in mistakes. Everything that has ever felt like a mistake always ends up as a positive outcome that I would not have anticipated. I believe everything is unfolding as it should, and that's what keeps me in the game each and every day.

Two

RAISING CAPITAL IS FUN (SAID NO ONE EVER)

Often when I speak to first-time entrepreneurs, I find they have one thing in common: they think of a successful fundraise as an end, rather than as a means to an end. Some even (foolishly) think of it as a reward. But when investors hand over a check, it's not a reward. A reward is a bonus. You don't give it back. Equity—the money you get from an investor or VC firm—is borrowed capital that has to be paid back . . . at a multiple.

Raising capital does not mean that you are successful, but based on the way a show such as *Shark Tank* portrays the fundraising process, you might assume that raising venture capital is like a fun game and kind of easy. It's definitely not. It's difficult and draining. Venture capitalists (VCs) cannot predict the future (despite their reputations), so they are not actually risk-takers. The best ones are just people who want to make sure they make as much money as possible on their investment. In fact, for every dollar a venture firm puts into an investment, it expects to get at least three dollars back, but aims to make seven to ten times what it put in. The stakes are high. For entrepreneurs, the stakes are even higher, as you're investing your time, your resources, and sometimes your own money.

This is why it's so important to make a clear pitch that shows the path to success. (We'll get to bouncing back from rejection later.) The good news is, if you know the secret to a great presentation, then you'll have leverage with investors. If not? You'll be operating blindly, and it's very likely investors will take advantage of you. So here's the one thing you need to do: raise money when you have power. Your power may be rooted in being the first mover in a growing market or—even better—a market that is yet to be created (think Uber or Square). Power can come from assembling a management team that has all of the requisite experience and know-how to make the business a knockout success. There is also power in having a product that meets a growing demand, requiring an immediate need for capital. Before I raised capital, I believed in "dumb money," or money that you could get from anyone if you had a good business plan. I didn't really think about building a huge business that required significant payback. After going through the process, I discovered that raising capital is about finding the right partners who can add significant value to help grow your business, including introductions to potential clients, industry knowledge, and increased brand awareness.

I started JOOR in the late summer of 2009. At that time, retailers bought goods from brands at tradeshows entirely on pen and paper. Having worked in the industry for several years, I knew there was a huge opportunity to transform the industry by moving wholesale selling online.

I started the business with my savings, and for two years I did not have a salary. In our first year, my goal was to prove that JOOR could sell its software to brands (who would use it to keep track of orders) and make money. If I could do that, then I knew I could eventually get retailers to pay for access to the platform to discover new brands and merchandise, and to budget and make purchases. Monetizing both sides of the market would show that JOOR could become a big business.

Before I went to the venture world, I believed that my power was my deep industry experience in luxury fashion and retail. That had helped me build up a roster of paying clients, and we were the first company to offer this software in the market. In order to realize my vision for JOOR, I would need more money to hire the team, rapidly acquire new customers, and add new software features.

I set out to raise $5 million so that I could scale the product and the team. The money would last us eighteen months and allow us to hit our revenue and customer-acquisition goals. My lawyer introduced me to five or six venture firms. Sometimes I pitched to senior venture-capital partners and other times to junior partners. A junior partner who wanted to make a mark in an all-white male firm pursued me. She had just lost a big fashion tech deal, and as a result, she was eager to make an investment in JOOR.

I signed a term sheet for $5 million (i.e., made a deal), but shortly after I signed it, the firm said I needed to hire two senior people in marketing, operations, or engineering before I would get the full five million. Instead, I was given a six-hundred-thousand-dollar convertible note, which is a loan that either converts to equity or debt, and the rest of the money was contingent on approval of those two partners. I believe this is called the old bait-and-switch move.

Because venture firms are deeply concerned about investment risk, they focused on my team's weakness: I didn't have a stellar management team (power fail!) in the eyes of the VC. It was just me and a few other junior members working on the business. I promptly hired a chief technology officer and a VP of marketing. But the partners of the firm were not impressed with these two hires. They wanted gray-haired (literally) babysitters—preferably the white male kind they had worked with in the past. They did not trust their junior partner *or* me. I also realized that the junior partner had very little power within the firm. She was focused on her promotion to partner and would bend over backward to please the senior partners in the firm.

I was dejected, but I didn't want to lose momentum, so I hired an executive search firm recommended by the venture firm and began a three-month search for a replacement CTO and another person to fill a C-level role. I narrowed the search down to two candidates and took them to meet all the venture capital partners. We re-pitched the business as a "team," hoping to impress the firm and get our capital.

Throughout the entire pitch meeting, the partners made jokes, passed notes back and forth, and stared at my legs. It was awkward for me but also for the two candidates that I had brought with me. They noticed it all. After the meeting they decided to back out of the project and suggested I do the same. Since they were seasoned leaders, they also gave me a warning that sounded like smart relationship advice: if the members of the venture firm were not respectful now, then, like in any long-term relationship, it would get worse. The two candidates walked away, and I was back to square one. I had to start my search again to get the deal done.

I went from thinking I was headed for success to being on the hook to the venture firm for $600,000—money that I needed to pay back in six months; otherwise they would take ownership of my company. So how did I feel? I had suddenly gone from knowing my power to feeling powerless.

I didn't know it at the time, but this was a pivotal moment. I had a choice in how I could view the situation (you always have a choice):

give up or find a way to gain my power back. Feeling used and abused was not my thing, so, with the help of my husband and two advisors, I worked through a plan to do that.

The first thing my company did was stop using the $600,000 the firm had given us. We had about $300,000 left, and we set that aside and didn't touch it. I started self-funding the company again, begging employees to be paid monthly rather than weekly. Deferring salaries of some of the senior people also helped to lessen my cash outlay.

Then I started calling people in my network just to share my story. I wanted to know whether what I had been through was "normal." It turns out it was not. I called other venture firms that liked to invest in early-stage companies. There is nothing more gratifying than going to a firm and telling your story about how one of their competitors tried to screw you, but I positioned myself as someone who wasn't going to be screwed in business or in life. On top of that, I was able to show the company was achieving solid metrics. My confidence proved to be attractive, and I found another venture firm to buy out the convertible note.

I was free. The VC that I ditched was pissed, and the junior partner was blindsided and probably lost her chance of getting promoted to partner. Splitting from the original VC firm was a big risk, but it felt great to take my power back. I was ready to give up the sleepless nights, the days of draining my funds to pay the salaries of twelve people, and living in fear.

By choosing to overcome obstacles rather than letting them hold us back we're able to expand our possibilities and potential. If you find yourself in a similar situation, try following these steps:

1.   **Socialize the problem.**

Have discrete conversations with people in your social and professional networks about how you're being treated, and figure out whether you should keep pursuing your path or go another route.

2. Be okay walking away.

Trust the process and have faith that things will work out. This was key for me.

3. Find a mantra and find a way.

This often-cited quote from Dale Carnegie, bestselling author and lecturer, propelled me forward: "Most of the important things in the world have been accomplished by people who kept on trying when there seemed to be no hope at all." I didn't want to be that entrepreneur, the one who is lazy or lacks the industriousness to find a solution to her financing problem.

Knowing your power is key when deciding whether you should pursue venture capitalists for financing, a bank for a small business loan, or help from friends and family. With the media glamorizing the venture world and almost making it seem like easy money, the consequences of taking venture capital is masked. It is absolutely not easy money, and the money will come with a pretty sizeable set of conditions. Asking yourself these three questions will help steer you toward or away from the venture world:

1. Can my business grow to $1 billion in value in seven to ten years?

2. Will I need more than $10 million to quickly scale and become the number-one player in my market?

3. Will I need to run the business at a loss for a few years to maintain market leadership and continue to grow quickly?

If you can answer yes to these three questions, then venture capital is the right option for you. If one or more of your answers is no, then think about why. Do you need just a few hundred thousand dollars to get to profitability? Because it might not be worth giving away 20 to 30 percent of your company to a venture capitalist for less than $1 million.

If you seek capital before you've found your power, you could end up facing a few issues. The first is the intangible. It's the smell of desperation. Investors typically do not initially pass on an investment because you lack revenue or your financial model is wonky. Many of the entrepreneurs I meet reek of desperation. Because you cannot define your power, you can't exude confidence. Let's be clear: it is not about exuding cockiness—that is a real turn-off. It is the silent confidence that says you know your business will be successful. If you do not believe in your own power, then you will not get others to buy in to your business either. After all of the meeting preparation, abundance of diligence, and countless data requests, venture capitalists will pass on your business. And once investors start passing on your business, news spreads. Once the word gets out that other investors have passed on investing in your business, then either your business won't get touched or VCs will prey on it.

Not finding your power can lead to other problems, especially when it comes to structuring deal terms. You'll end up with one-sided employment letters, dilution preferences (no protection from your stock from diluting when additional stock is issued), lack of pro rata rights (inability to participate in subsequent rounds of funding so that you can maintain your ownership percentage), and other things that give the VC unbalanced control of your company. With this asymmetry of power, it will get harder and harder for you to keep your rights as a founder. Bottom line: you'll have more power if you educate yourself on deal terms, and knowledge will help you keep a level head when you feel excited about landing an investment.

Founders willing to sign away their company by giving away a large chunk of equity are obviously either underestimating demand or just trying to pursue money believing that there are no strings attached. When you know your power—and have confidence in the worth of your business—then you can make smarter decisions about how to fund your business and how much equity you should be willing to give away. Make this your mantra, and write it on a sticky note at your desk: "Do not raise money in times of need—raise money when you know your power."

Inside Story
Interview with Sasha Plavsic, Founder and Chief Creative Officer of ILIA Beauty, the Pioneer Clean-Beauty Brand Founded in 2011

The philosophy behind ILIA grew from Sasha's desire to understand the ingredients on the back of a ChapStick box. Through trial and error, Sasha used her experience from working at a branding firm called Tank Design, a brief stint freelancing at Urban Decay Cosmetics and at the re-branded Saje Natural Wellness, combined with her history of sensitive skin, to develop skincare and makeup formulas that would help rejuvenate and heal. Today ILIA is sold in more than twenty countries and offers more than 120 SKUs and twenty products.

I interviewed Sasha to understand why she waited several years to raise capital. I learned how she thinks about her power in the market and why she decided to hire an outside CEO to help grow her business.

1.   **What was your motivation for launching ILIA?**

The neuron that fired within me to start ILIA happened when I came back to North America after several years of living in Europe. I moved back home with my parents at the age of thirty and had a bit of a crisis. When I moved home, I was cleaning out my makeup bag, and my mother made me think twice about what I was putting on my face and body. So I started doing research on the ingredients in makeup and skincare. I became frustrated with the lack of transparency around the ingredients in some of my favorite makeup and skin-care brands.

My product inspiration was a tinted European lip balm I'd been using for half my life. I really loved that product but wanted to create a cleaner, organic-based version of it. It took me two years to develop a truly comparable product.

2. **When you were getting your business off the ground, how did you fund your business?**

My fundraising journey is different than many other beauty brands. ILIA is eight years old. We are not a young company. We didn't do our first capital raise until last year. When I started experimenting with clean beauty in 2011, I didn't have a business plan. I just started learning and defining what clean beauty meant to me. I used two credit cards, and my father cosigned a bank loan for another $25,000. It cost $35,000 to launch, and we continued bootstrapping the business with minimal investment over the next few years.

3. **I read that ILIA raised funding from a VC firm in December 2018. Can you talk about how much you raised and the fundraising process?**

We were fortunate enough to raise what was needed at the time for a minority investment. We had multiple offers from firms, but we went with one that would be the best partner and could add the most value. We wanted investors who had built direct-to-consumer business and understood the retail side of beauty. I think we held off for a long time to get our business in order. It doesn't really make sense to go out and raise capital when so many aspects of our business were still being figured out.

4.   What things did you feel like you needed to figure out?

We had to design our competitive advantage over the last few years. The first advantage is inherent to our first-mover advantage. I've been told by many of our retail partners that we were one of the first clean-color brands to the industry. Second, we needed to develop a full product assortment. Today, we have a full array of SKUs (eighty-five) on a one-bay presentation (on a four-shelf gondola) at Sephora. Third, we needed to build the right team. I didn't have experience in beauty. I stumbled upon this opportunity through my own needs and desires. Today, we have an amazing team spearheaded by a CEO, Lynda Berkowitz, whom I brought into the business three years ago. Her experience spans over twenty years in beauty. Next, we have a robust product pipeline. We have developed a specific and unique way to formulate products. It took me many years to develop and refine our methodology. Figuring these things out was super critical before we raised any outside capital.

5.   Given your own journey, what advice do you have for founders looking to raise capital?

My advice to founders is bootstrap as long as you can. Also, for us it would have been way harder to raise funds when clean beauty wasn't even a trend a few years ago. The timing for clean beauty just started a year ago. Timing is everything with investors. They have to feel like demand is imminent.

6.   **It kind of sounds like you were reluctant to take on outside funding. What was your real motivation to do so?**

I think consumer businesses should think about bank loans or lines of credit. It doesn't make sense to give a portion of your company away to investors, especially when you are small, and equity is expensive when you are funding an inventory-based business. Also, you want to retain control over your business. After all, you are the one building it day after day. We were getting money from the banks, but it wasn't enough capital. As we grew we needed to explore other channels. But if you can rely on debt funding, I think that is better, as you don't have to start giving your company away to others—yet.

7.   **When you were fundraising, did anyone say no?**

The only ones who said no to us were the venture funds that wanted the check size to be larger. That's another tip for entrepreneurs: you shouldn't raise more money than you need. And you certainly don't want to be a speck in the sand, or a speck in a crown of jewels. Meaning, if you are too small or not growing fast enough, then the investors will probably spend less time with you. You don't want to raise a lot of money too soon.

8.   **Raising capital seemed like an easy process for you. Was it?**

It was easy because we raised at the right time and were clear about our value proposition. The trend for clean beauty was reaching a tipping point. We had figured a lot of issues out in our business model. I hired a strong CEO who is a veteran in the space. So we were firing on all cylinders in terms of strong team, product, and market opportunity. But a lot of people—especially women—say, "You are so lucky that you created your own business. I want to do that." And I respond by saying you have to be built like steel to be an entrepreneur. It's difficult to have it all. When I am at work, I miss out on my kids. When I am with my kids, I am missing out on something at work. There is no guarantee that I will still be doing this forever. I have to fight for playing in this role every day.

9.   What has been the biggest challenge for you to overcome?

The comparison culture in the US is challenging. We are all comparing ourselves to others. It's the Instagram culture. I am Canadian and my husband is from Holland, and it's a different mentality where we grew up. As an entrepreneur, you have to stay true to your original mission and have conviction. It's important to know what the competition is up to, but you can't get caught up in that too much. It's important to look ahead and at the same time be aware of what's happening around you; just don't let it take all of your energy.

10.   Is there a specific example of when you hit a low point? How did you overcome it?

Before I hired my CEO, I felt like I was under water. I literally stopped breathing in so many situations. We were experiencing a lot of issues, including considerable production issues. I realized in those moments that I had to hire people so that I could have space to work on the vision of the business. Without a vision there is no business. I happened to be a new mom, and I could no longer sustain the eight a.m. to one a.m. workday. It was a difficult time for me. I was not doing great at so many things.

I truly believe that you can only be great in two areas of your life. Attempting to do more doesn't really allow you to be great or even good at anything. For me, I want to be a great mom and a great product visionary. I realized that I needed to get out of my own way to do so. I also learned that it's how you build a company and who you do it with that is the ultimate sign of success.

...

Sasha's story is about knowing your power at all times. It's in your hands from the beginning, and once you've figured out the point of strength for your business, it's important to find the right venture-capital match (not just anyone willing to give you money). Think about which investors are seeking the power you possess. Can you find ones who have not yet invested in your industry and want to round their portfolios? Are there any who want to invest in more female founders, and your well-rounded management team would add diversity they need? Figure out what need you can fill. And remember to think of capital as a means to fuel your business so that you can succeed faster. Once you do, you'll be able to pay back what you promised investors—and then some.

THREE

No Means Not Right Now

In order to raise capital quickly, I learned the hard way that it's important to de-risk your company for investors. Does your sales cycle take a long time? If your lead time to land a customer is months, or even years, then you need to provide a plan for how to shorten it. Does your product fit the market that you want to serve, or do you have a long pipeline of things you need to build before you start landing customers? Are you seeing user and revenue growth? It's important to bring in revenue, but a revenue-growth trajectory is what shows your company has promise. It's important to take these fundamentals seriously. If not, you might be successful in raising capital, but the growth process will be painful.

Here are a few more questions to ask yourself before you go after coveted venture dollars: Are you thinking as big as your investors? Will your business make money and scale? And most importantly, are you ready to grow your business quickly? Investors are looking for massive revenue growth—meaning that your top-line sales should grow to at least three or four times your prior year's revenue. The belief is that once a company becomes big enough (think Amazon), then it has enough of the pieces of the puzzle figured out to shift to profitability with time.

Assuming you have a strong understanding of what it takes to raise capital and scale, then your next goal is to ensure that you're in the best mind-set when you're selling clients, pitching investors, and wooing potential new hires. To prepare, you need to know your vision, business model, and sales pitch like the back of your hand. You want your presentation to sound effortless. Do not underestimate the amount of time it will take to internalize your pitch. Get your selling points down, and then practice repeating your pitch over and over again until your delivery feels completely natural.

When I first pitched clients, I would wing the meeting. I thought I could talk my way through any situation. After being rejected several times, I started to practice my pitch at least fifty times in advance of my meetings. Being practiced afforded me the ability to handle any comments, questions, or unexpected scenarios that were thrown at me during the discussion. Sometimes my audience would take control, and I needed to change direction. Knowing my pitch allowed me to read the room and get a sense of the energy of the audience so that I could alter my approach as needed. I began to create notecards for every slide of a presentation, each containing three bullet points: what I wanted to say to introduce the slide, the main point of the slide, and the lead-in to the next slide.

In the beginning, I did a poor job anticipating all of the questions I would be asked, from the basic "How much money do you need to get to profitability?" to the inappropriate "How do you juggle your kids with your start-up?" Many times people pitching a business idea rely on a slew of slides tacked onto the end of the presentation. Then, when a question is asked, many take five minutes sifting through the background materials or scrolling through a financial model. Know your backup information cold too. I started to relish meetings with people who would ask me tough questions, because instead of feeling like my business (or I) wasn't good enough, I was grateful that these people were inadvertently preparing me for my next big meeting. That positive mind-set gave me the stamina to keep going.

During some meetings, there were times when I was terrified because I didn't know the answer to a question. I'd often try to fake a response or divert the conversation to a slightly different topic. It felt disingenuous. One important lesson I learned is that you don't need an answer for everything. Obviously, it would be nice to crush all the questions—and that means not being afraid to say, "I don't know that answer, but I'll look into it and get back to you." In many instances, investors or potential clients are not testing for knowledge; rather, they're testing for humility and honesty. Investors listen to hundreds of pitches a year; they have a good instinct for when someone is trying to pull the wool over their eyes.

Once I started to feel more than prepared delivering my pitch, I learned that I needed to have the right energy to really sell it. When you're pitching to a potential partner—be it a client, investor, or new hire—remember the things your mom told you as a kid: exude tempered excitement, make eye contact, stand up straight, and keep smiling. I do my best work when people sense my passion, and if I am excited, then I can get my audience excited.

The next step was to get my tone right. I learned to speak evenly while punctuating my key points—the things I wanted my audience to remember. Oftentimes I would speak quickly because I noticed that my clients and investors were distracted by their phones or email. I also pause occasionally so the audience can ask questions or respond to my questions.

Often investors have "good cops" (people who seem friendly and supportive) and "bad cops" (the ones who challenge you on everything) in a meeting room. Another thing that really helped my presentations was I stopped assuming the "bad cops" were out to get me. In reality, they are looking to see how you will react when you, your team, and your business model are pressure-tested, so try not to let them rattle you or take their attitudes personally.

No matter what happens, you want to end all your meetings on a high note. Also, don't leave without mutually agreed upon next steps (that you fully understand), especially when it comes to pitching possible customers. This will give you a reason to follow up—you never want to lose momentum after an important meeting. I learned that following up within seventy-two hours is imperative to getting to the next step or closing a deal. As more time lapses, it becomes less likely either will get done.

After the meeting, digest your audience's questions and come up with ways to improve your pitch and responses to questions. Sometimes reordering slides or changing your takeaways in the presentation to stress key points that didn't come across is helpful. You should be continually fine-tuning things.

After all of this prepping and planning, you still might get a "no" from a client, investor, or potential new hire. The first thing to understand is that no doesn't mean no forever. It means not right now. It certainly burns when someone says no. That little word can have such a big impact. It bruises your ego, it might dampen your energy, and it's certainly exasperating because you have to try again. Nevertheless, your job at that point is to try to get as much feedback as possible—this is where you can learn (and grow) the most.

In the thousands of sales pitches that I've made in the last ten years, I've learned to welcome the times I hear "no." I would ask myself a lot of questions after the meeting. I go through a series of questions such as, What are the main reasons for the "no"? If they were to see me again in six months, what would they want to see changed? Is there anybody else in their network that I should talk to further? If I didn't have the answers, I would ask the client or investor in a follow-up call.

Rejection is tough. Repeated rejection is even harder. How do you keep going? And how do you know when to give up? The first thing to do is to stop thinking that you are not good enough or that your business is not good enough. The negativity in your head can be difficult to stop. The worst way to get stuck is to focus on one particular failure and assume failure will result in other areas of your life.

When I first launched my software business, over a dozen potential clients rejected me. I knew my pitch and product had to improve. "No" meant that my product-market fit was just not right. It was so easy to feel embarrassed and stop meeting with clients. But I kept going. Companies in the fashion industry can be really tough, to the point where they are snide and rude. I learned to stop taking things personally. I was determined to get answers so that I could get my pitch right.

I've found it's really helpful to make a list of everything I intend to accomplish in a client meeting. Then I check off everything I accomplished. This gives me a visual representation of what I do right and what I still have to master—and it helps me move forward. The second thing I do is accept responsibility. I make a list of the mistakes I made and then figure out how to internalize those lessons so I don't make the same mistakes in the next pitch. The last thing I do is try to remember that if I learn from every rejection, it gets me one step closer to reaching my goal.

Inside Story
Interview with Sarah Kauss, Founder and Chief Executive Officer of S'well

Sarah Kauss is the founder and CEO of S'well, a.k.a. the creator of the original chic water bottle that has become a must-have accessory. With S'well, which she launched in 2010, she married her passion for fashion, hydration, and philanthropy to disrupt the reusable bottle industry and transform the on-the-go drinking experience. I talked to Sarah about the mind tricks that worked for her, how she handled rejection, and how she managed to grow her business to $100 million in sales in nine years without taking any outside capital.

1. **In the early days, how did you mentally get ready for a client pitch?**

It was with a great deal of optimism. I had no doubts about the ability of S'well bottles to change the world for good, but I also knew that I was small and needed to be bigger than I was to grow faster. My apartment turned into "my office," and my parents turned into "my team." Changing my lens on the situation, these were just little ways to help me remember that this wasn't just a hobby, but a business.

2. **Can you describe a time when a potential client said no?**

Bloomingdale's said no for two years. They kept telling me they didn't carry water bottles, and I kept saying, "But these are hydration fashion accessories." They eventually came around to see my side of things. During that time, I never felt dejected. I so believed in what this bottle represented and could do that I knew it was only a matter of time. Even when my accountant suggested that I get a "real" job, I didn't feel rejected. I simply knew that I had a good idea and that I needed to talk to more potential customers to help get it off the ground. Failure was not an option for me.

3. How did you handle those feelings?

I'm an eternal optimist. And I believed in what I was doing, that there was no way a "no" could get me down. I just figured I wasn't talking to the right person or they needed more time to come around. I kept taking action and would not let the rejection deter me.

4. How did you process the feedback that you got from retailers who first said no?

I knew my story about why I wanted this water bottle was authentic, and that there had to be others out there who had a similar need as me—people who wanted to have a bottle that looked beautiful and performed. I tried to turn any rejection or even lack of traction into learnings. And I used it to fuel my determination to make them say *yes*. Belief in myself and my idea were critical to continuing to move forward, and my persistence paid off.

5. Your optimism is infectious, but can you describe an experience when you needed to get realistic about something in your business that wasn't working?

When I first launched S'well, you would have thought we were a nonprofit. A nonprofit that happened to be selling bottles, instead of a for-profit reusable-bottle company. I was highlighting the problem of single-use plastic waste. I wasn't doing a good job showing all of the benefits of the product that I wanted to sell, and in turn my bottles weren't selling. I needed to shift the story to resonate better with my customers.

6. How did that feedback improve your subsequent pitches?

This feedback helped me really nail down the positioning for the brand. It helped me understand that I couldn't lead with the problem that I wanted to solve—ridding the world of plastic bottles—but rather with how S'well can improve the customer's experience through beauty and performance. It also helped me eventually understand that fashion was critical to our messaging and how leveraging fashion would help the company evolve.

7. When you're pursuing a goal, how do you know when to stay the course or to quit? What analysis do you use to decide?

Data, such as sales numbers and consumer insights, is essential, but so too is trusting my gut. Even when I didn't have data, I thought of myself as the consumer—what would I need or desire? Over the years, we've led with design and gut while listening to our customers. They love to share thoughts on social media or directly with our customer service team. We've used that feedback to develop new products and accessories, such as our wide-mouth Travelers, large-format Roamers, and drink-through caps, among other items. These allow our customers to use S'well products in new and interesting ways, all while enhancing their on-the-go lifestyle.

8. What is the hardest challenge you've had to overcome?

This might sound crazy, but growing as fast as we did, I like to say that we were flying the airplane while building it. From 2012 to 2016, we saw an amazing amount of growth, going from a two-million-dollar company to a hundred-million-dollar company. We didn't necessarily have the team or the resources in place and had to be resourceful with how we delivered quality and met demand.

9.   How did you handle your rapid growth? What were the most pressing changes you had to make?

We reset. We put foundational elements in place on the operational level to make sure we could deliver for long-term growth. This meant evolving the team by adding senior talent in areas like sales, marketing, and production; building out back-end support; and changing vendors to ones that could handle and scale with our growing demand.

10.   What is the one thing you think every entrepreneur should believe?

My conversation is always around moving forward perfectly imperfect. Early on, I was so focused on being perfect that it slowed me down. I realized that I could have evolved the business faster if I'd let more people in on my idea. My advice: don't wait until you feel that your idea is perfect to share it with your trusted network or the public. It will inevitably change and evolve once the world is interacting with it. Give it the chance to get better, faster. The fact of the matter is that if you're putting yourself out there, pushing boundaries, doing what you believe in, you're already on your way to greatness.

Four

Have a Go-To Market
Strategy or Go Home

I talk with ten to fifteen entrepreneurs every month. I review their investor presentations, advise them on strategy, and determine whether I want to invest my own capital in their businesses. I always zone in on an entrepreneur's go-to market strategy. This strategy entails how they plan to get customers to buy their product or service. What gets me every time is that the slides are almost always generic. Nine times out of ten I see bullets stating they will create ads on Facebook and Instagram stories, partner with influencers, get on billboards, place subway ads, and buy keywords for search engine optimization (SEO).

Most investor pitches are devoid of creative solutions for how to get into the hearts and minds of customers. When I press founders on their customer-adoption plan, they usually say the proceeds of a loan or equity raise will go toward hiring a chief marketing officer or a vice president of digital marketing. It's disheartening. Many of the best CEOs would also make the best chief marketing officers at any company (think Lauren Hobart at Dick's Sporting Goods or Jay Farner at Quicken Loans). As a business owner, your job is to figure out how to get your target customer to purchase your product or service with ease. If you cannot articulate how you're going to conquer your share of the market, it sends a signal to investors that you are not prepared to rapidly scale. When founders expect someone else on the team to find the silver bullet, it's a major red flag.

Having a solid grasp on the fundamental difference between basic tactics and a real marketing strategy is imperative for any entrepreneur. Relying on Facebook ads and Instagram stories is a tactic. Spending money on Facebook and influencers is a tactic. They are levers the company will pull to create, market, and sell their product. A strategy is a one- to two-year plan for how a business will get closer to its vision, win against competitors, and get closer to achieving its ten-year vision.

For example, if a software company's goal is "to become the number-one productivity software provider in the world," the tactics would be the levers the company will pull to create, market, and sell this type of software. The company strategy, meanwhile, might be "to create software that maximizes employee productivity," such as developing programs that compete with Excel, email, and similar database applications.

Since hiring talent to figure out your business strategy *for* you is never the only answer, you need to spend time planning out your ten-year vision. Break down your vision into manageable pieces by first outlining three or four strategies that will help you reach your goal—each strategy should only take you one to two years to achieve. Then, come up with the tactics (levers you can pull) to help make it all happen.

Here's an example of what I mean. It's an example that applies to a direct-to-consumer business.

Vision *(Your Destination or Dream)*	Strategy *(Goals to Your Vision)*	Tactics *(Your Actions)*
Become the world's leading natural producer of premium food products and best-in-class services that exceed our customers' tastes and desires.	Year 1 to Year 3: Get known for having the best-in-breed products made at the best manufacturing facilities in North America.	1. Create a narrow line of products, and manufacture them at third-party facilities. 2. Start selling products to build brand awareness at three major retailers. 3. Research and design best-in-class production plants. 4. Raise $50 million to build two manufacturing facilities. 5. Spend $5 million on advertising (social, billboards).
	Year 4 to Year 7: Purchase farms to grow organic, pesticide-free ingredients, and expand product line to include three to four new categories.	1. Build manufacturing facilities. 2. Raise $100 million to purchase two farms and necessary equipment. 3. Hire team to support the addition of new categories, manufacturing plants, and farms. 4. Spend $10 million on expanded advertising programs (social, radio, billboards, TV, podcasts).
	Year 7 to Year 10: Open own stores in twenty-five cities that exclusively sell our branded product.	1. Raise $200 million to open stores in key cities. 2. Create unique shopping experience based on luxury and convenience. 3. Hire best customer service team to service customers in store. 4. Spend $20 million on advertising.

In this case, the long-term vision does not really change over time. It is this vision that gets you out of bed in the morning. Your vision needs to have the same effect on your team: it needs to motivate them to work as hard as you do. It is your business's promise to the world.

When I work with an entrepreneur, I ask her to map out her strategies and brainstorm the tactics that will allow for success. I tell her to list out as many tactics as she can. Typically, I've found that after listing the first five or ten ideas, she thinks she's found the answers and then stops. But I make her come up with forty to fifty more. When she's finally done, I have her circle the five or ten she believes will most likely achieve her strategic objectives.

The tactics should be considered flexible. That's why businesses that don't measure anything rarely succeed. If key performance indicators are in place, then your metrics will tell you whether your tactics are getting you closer to achieving your strategic objectives. Changing your tactics is a natural—and important—part of business. It is the constant innovation of your tactics that stimulates team creativity and motivates employees to come up with their best ideas.

I've done this exercise with teams countless times, and the same thing happens. This is what I've learned is true:

1. The first five to ten tactics are generic—some tactics will work, and some will not because they are stale ideas.

2. Creativity really comes when you push yourself to come up with as many tactics as you can—to go beyond what is comfortable when brainstorming.

3. The Pareto Principle truly applies to this exercise: 20 percent of the tactics listed will allow you to achieve at least 80 percent of your strategic goal.

The need for resilience comes into play when your tactics are not working. For example, in business you could be spending a lot of money on billboards and subway ads, but your market share is not increasing. The tactics are not getting you closer to achieving your strategic objectives. We've all been there. So what often happens? Many beat themselves up because they believe they don't have enough willpower. Others give up, throwing in the towel altogether, thinking that there is no hope. But most people come up with a reason why they aren't "enough" to succeed.

I use a different approach.

When I start working on a tactic, I simultaneously map out the expected outcome. If I don't achieve it, I simply change the tactic. I don't view it as a failure. I simply view it as an outcome I was not expecting, and I figure out another tactic to try next. I keep doing and re-doing this process, never labeling it as a failure—just as an outcome I do not want. This framework helps me move faster instead of getting hung up on the "failure" and attaching emotion around the process.

Your mind-set is crucial when it comes to thinking about your tactical successes and failures. You need a mantra to help you bounce back quickly and avoid passing the blame on to others or yourself.

Inside Story
Interview with Stephen Kuhl, Cofounder and Chief Executive Officer of Burrow

Stephen is the cofounder and CEO of Burrow, a start-up that's reinventing the furniture industry. In 2018, Burrow was named one of the ten most innovative retail brands in the world by Fast Company, and the Burrow sofa was named of the fifty best inventions of the year by *TIME* magazine. Stephen discusses how he rebounded from a failed go-to market approach.

1.   What is your long-term vision for Burrow?

Our vision is to reinvent the furniture industry by offering clever, comfortable, and long-lasting furniture, shipping the same week that it's ordered, with an unparalleled customer experience. Our strategy was first to spend two or three years targeting our customer's living room. We have accomplished that. Now our customers are asking for more. So we will spend the next couple years going after the broader home, and then we will pursue building for the entire home. For each of these strategies we have a bunch of tactics that we employ, such as finding the best quality suppliers at the lowest costs. Once we achieve our goals, then we move to the next strategy. It's like taking a giant step every two or three years.

2.   When you set out to tackle "owning the living room," were there any tactics you used that didn't work?

In 2018 we raised our Series A. During our seed stage, we ran advertising tests in a bunch of marketing channels. Paid social, press, word of mouth, and paid search were all marketing channels that were working. We were ready to fuel rapid growth with the money we raised. We put a lot of pressure on ourselves and went after seven or eight channels. And we foolishly thought all of them were going to work. We tested connected TV, radio ads, and USPS's MyMove mailers. We spent 10 percent of our marketing spend on those additional channels, which was about $100,000 a month. And they failed.

3.   So then what did you do?

When channels don't work, then your metrics look terrible. Your customer-acquisition costs are terribly high, and your revenue is lower than you thought it would be. And your investors are saying, "What is happening?" It was a really challenging time for us. We had to dig deep and find a way to make ground back up. We focused on the marketing channels that we knew worked and stopped experimenting with radio and television.

4.   Did you stop regretting the mistake?

Sometimes self-doubt creeps in. I wonder, Do I not have enough belief in my vision? Am I not good enough as a leader? Or am I putting way too much pressure on the team? Am I hard to say no to? Can they not stand up to me? I've learned to overcome some of this internal talk by asking a lot of questions to our team. If you don't talk to the team and really get beneath the surface, then it's a guessing game. Is the setback something that is internal or external? You start internally and then move externally by asking questions to the team.

5.   How did you get out of your head in this particular case?

There is a lot of noise that happens in your head. Are we not a strong enough team? Are we failing? How much of the noise do you believe? Failure, especially in a team setting, does test you because you need to work through issues together and are forced to go back and analyze together. You have to figure out, Is it the team, the stuff we did as a team, or is it the tactic itself? That process of unearthing what the source of the setback is can be grueling to replay. Success spoils you, and you don't become as discerning. But, ultimately, you have to believe that failure is good and it's how you get better. Also, we are careful about how we talk about things as a team. So for instance, we don't say that radio advertising doesn't work for us. Instead we say, no, radio didn't work for us *today*. It is a very likely possibility that radio will work when our company gets bigger or when we make our radio spending a different ratio to our overall marketing spend. We, as a team, are getting better about evaluating failures and how we talk about them.

6.   When you see that a tactic is successful, what is the hardest part of execution?

As a founder, you are wearing a lot of hats. There are three buckets in your work: things you are good at, things you are bad at, and things you don't know how to do. That goes for your team too. In the beginning, things tend to work out because it's a smaller team, and you, as CEO, can manage every work stream that is happening in the office. As you grow the team, it gets harder and harder to manage the execution. That's when setbacks can blindside you. Things are moving, but you can't control everything.

7.   How did this experience change the way you approach things today?

Before I even start something, I need to define what success looks like. If we do this, and it does X or Y, then will we continue or will we stop? It takes the guesswork out of the equation. It's easier when *I* am doing the task, because I trust that I've properly exhausted everything I can think of to make this thing work. It's harder when others are doing it. You have to ask a lot of questions. You have to figure out the right questions to ask people. Why is it not working? What did you try? What was the order of operations? You have to ask: Why? Why? Why?

8. So how are you turning Burrow's vision into a reality?

When we originally started we didn't have a grand vision. We wanted to build good product. Now, after we have confidence under our belt, our vision is getting more and more ambitious. There is no reason why we can't have the design and development principles that Apple does. In the beginning you can't always see the possibilities. You have to prove it to yourself, taking baby steps every day. Now we ask ourselves, But why can't we be a one-billion-dollar business? We actually can, because we have the confidence. The confidence to take action.

9. Where do you find inspiration for your products?

When you have success, you attract successful people. It's like gravity. People that you looked up to somehow get sucked into your orbit. We attracted the CEO of a large furniture manufacturer. He called us up and told us that we will be a two-billion-dollar company in ten years, and he wants to manufacture our furniture for us. Most of my days are filled with minutiae, and sometimes it's hard to focus on the bigger picture. But some days you have a conversation about the true potential of your business, and you feel rejuvenated and validated.

10. Who do you surround yourself with to inspire you to realize your vision?

I don't have a lot of peers that I talk to. We have different advisors who provide tactical and industry guidance. We have investors who ask us how we are doing. But finding people who can think big is important. We have one advisor we brainstorm with and feel rejuvenated. Every day and all day long I hear about problems and get told no over and over again. I'm around so much negativity. It's easy to get sucked into that thinking. You have to proactively train yourself to what is possible. It is a concerted effort in thinking optimistically. One way we do this is to focus on the "Yes . . . and" rather than the "No . . . but." Rather than pointing out all the things that can go wrong with an idea, we say YES first AND we expound on the idea. This gets us to think freely and creatively.

. . .

Through my discussion with Stephen, I realized that knowing your *why* is a critical component for ensuring success. For instance, many people say they would like to achieve financial independence, but after a few months or weeks of curbing spending, they lose sight of their *why* or don't have the willpower to stick to their goals.

The *why* takes a few iterations to find. If achieving financial independence is your thing, the *why* might be because you want to travel the world with your husband while you are still young. That *why* has to be so compelling that it gets you fired up no matter what. There also has to be *pain* associated with not achieving your *why*. For example, "If I don't achieve financial independence by the age of sixty, I will risk not being able to travel the world because everyone in my family has passed on by the age of seventy, and that could happen to me." Dire, I know. Motivating? Yes.

When thinking about your *why*, figure out what you will miss out on if you don't achieve it. Ask yourself what it will cost you if you don't reach your goal. If you do achieve your vision, what is the upside? What doors will it open? What will it mean to the world and to your community?

Ultimately, if you want to fulfill your vision, then you want to be what I call "decided." Then you're fully committed to going through pain or heartache—whatever it takes. You have full grasp of what will happen if you don't push forward. There's no longer a voice inside your head that needs to coax you to get up and start your day, because the drive has become ingrained. Your drive is part of who you are. When you're decided, you know in your heart of hearts that your vision will be realized.

FIVE

TOUGH-LOSS RECOVERY: LOSING KEY TEAM MEMBERS

For any business owner, building the right team is critical to success. But no matter how well you pay, or how many free snacks or vacation days you provide, you are never fully in control of your employees' happiness. They can leave at any time and for any reason. Learning to deal with that—not to mention finding and recruiting people who are invested in what you are building, especially when things get tough—is so important. I have learned that team change, no matter how painful or unexpected, can be a good thing.

As a nontechnical founder, starting a software company was challenging for me. Possessing industry expertise and forming professional relationships are necessary for landing clients, but without a great product, your relationships and industry know-how won't be enough to give you a competitive advantage. The power of your software is what will ultimately keep you in business. Great designers and software engineers, however, are in short supply. And with tech titans such as Facebook and Google offering cushy jobs with significant starting salaries, it is hard to compete. You know this for certain when an engineer you've hired—who has barely two years' experience—jumps ship for a high-profile start-up and a fifty-thousand-dollar pay raise.

That's not the only challenge when it comes to technical talent. Finding talented engineers who are interested in the problem you are trying to solve isn't always easy, and neither is finding ones who can develop great chemistry with your business team. You see, business and tech people don't always mix well. Entrepreneurs are known to be dominant, pie-in-the-sky individuals who are constantly navigating the highs and lows of building their businesses. We can be impatient and not the clearest communicators when it comes to ironing out the details. Software engineers usually prefer proper pacing, persistence, and steadiness. The holy grail in landing your perfect employee is finding the triumvirate of good chemistry, requisite skill set, and passion for the job.

As eager as you may be to get your business moving forward, I've learned from experience that it's never a good idea to rush the hiring process. It takes time to determine whether someone is the right fit for a role—that could mean a thorough interview a process that could last one to two months. This is one of the hardest parts of building your company! Even if a candidate's past experiences sound similar to what you need her to do, there's no guarantee she will be a rock-star performer in your unique culture and environment. The qualities you are looking for are often intangible, but what you (and the other team members involved in the hiring process) should suss out is whether a candidate has enthusiasm for the role, whether there's chemistry with the other employees, and how the candidate would handle situations specific to your business.

For better or worse, you'll probably learn relatively quickly if a new hire isn't the right fit, and my advice is to part ways quickly if that's the case. Still, after a painstaking interview and recruiting process, losing key team members is heartbreaking and can really affect team morale. Sometimes, when an employee is such an embedded part of your team, there will be a domino effect, and one or two others will depart at the same time. There can be a herd mentality in the start-up world, and you may discover that some employees are loyal to the soon-to-be departed, or they realize they can get a higher salary elsewhere, or they just want to work for the shiniest new start-up in town.

Over the years, I've lost several key members (heads of product and of engineering) for various other reasons too. Either the hours were too long, the work was not a match with their skill sets, or the office culture was a bad fit. My feelings around a team member's departure ranged from amicable to downright nasty. No matter what, the loss always stung. I always felt like I was being abandoned. And when you lose key members at a critical juncture in your business—during large product launches, after closing a big client, or while you are about to close a big fundraising round—it can feel demoralizing. It's the worst when you have to let clients or new investors know that a person critical to their decision is no longer with the company.

When this happened to me, I'd feel a lot of hurt and regret. I would retreat inward and dwell on how everything unfolded—playing and replaying in my head how I could have approached the relationship with the employee differently. I'd think about how much our company had sacrificed for that individual—the time spent interviewing him, onboarding him, and training him. That would often be on top of external training classes, pay raises, and generous compensation. And now he's deserting the team?

The hurt often turned into anger, and then the self-doubt seeped in. I would wonder if I had done something wrong. Could I have acted differently during a particular conflict? Could I have provided more business context around the importance of that team member's work? Should we have spent more time together? It felt a lot like a bad romantic breakup.

To overcome the onslaught of emotion, I'd always jump into action quickly. After all, when a key player leaves, there's a lot to do: break the news to the team, conduct an exit interview, transition projects, promote someone from within, or hire someone new. And you still have to keep up with your usual responsibilities. Expect to feel daunted and weary—you now have all these problems you didn't anticipate.

Instead of getting trapped into feeling sorry for yourself, you need to focus on how you're going to move forward—and, more importantly, move your team forward. It cannot possibly be the end of the world. Other businesses have lost key team members and have gone on to be successful.

So how do you get over your internal hurdles and shift your mind-set? It personally took me several years to figure out how to psychologically deal with team departures. Business is ultimately a people-based endeavor. That's why it's easy to take things personally. Instead of letting myself or the team feel the loss, I wanted to fill the role and move past the pain. In retrospect, that wasn't the right thing to do. I should have struck a better balance between feeling sad the person was leaving and feeling energized the business would move forward. Perhaps even some new ways of doing business would emerge.

If I have one big regret, it's that when I ran my start-up, I didn't do a great job acknowledging people's feelings, and I was exceptionally bad at allowing people to leave in a graceful way. I found it difficult to take the high road and simply wish folks well as they departed. I often resented people for not having the stamina and smarts needed for a nascent company, or for leaving us in a lurch. What's worse, I made leaving a difficult experience because I thought that would make people stay. Counterintuitive, I know. I learned the hard way that letting people leave graciously makes the whole team feel better about the loss, and it allows everyone else to get closure faster. It's inevitable that things will change, and you just have to accept that employees will always come and go. If I could go back in time and do it all over again, rather than spending so much of my mental energy on being mad and questioning why people leave, I should have been creating a company environment that embraced personnel changes. As the saying goes, "Even when a superstar leaves, the moon will still shine."

Turnover and retention was one of my top organizational challenges at JOOR because I didn't build a strong culture from the get-go. I was in the wrong frame of mind when dealing with loss. Over time, I retrained my mind to believe that things happen for a reason. My talk track was, "No need to worry; the best is yet to come."

The truth is, departures should always be viewed as an opportunity to shake things up. Instead of action so you can replace someone as quickly as possible, take a minute to think about alternatives. Roles can be rejiggered and responsibilities can get split up. Team members can be promoted from within. Sometimes, reorganizing the staff (or any kind of shakeup) can accelerate change. It's bound to happen anyway, so just remember that how you handle it is what's most important. Surviving the ups and downs of scaling a business means leaving any fear-based mind-set behind and getting excited about a future filled with new opportunities.

Inside Story
An Interview with Annie Jackson, Cofounder and Chief Operating Officer of Credo Beauty

Beauty veteran Annie Jackson has been a quintessential element in the success of some of the undoubtedly biggest beauty meccas on the planet, including Sephora, Benefit, and Estée Lauder. Annie's love of beauty and her quest for cleaner options led her to create Credo Beauty. She and her cofounder, Shashi Batra, shared a vision to change the way people think about what they put in and on their bodies and skin. A professional merchant, Annie has not just created a new generation of beauty brands that are natural, organic, effective, clean, and green, she has literally started a clean-beauty movement in retail. In 2016, Shashi, the company's CEO, was diagnosed with lung cancer; sadly, he lost his battle eight months later. Annie, who took over as CEO, discusses how she moved through the loss and how her team came back even stronger with new hires on board, and reinvigorated team morale.

1. **In May 2017, you lost your cofounder and dear friend, Shashi Batra. Tell me how Shashi's death impacted your business.**

When Shashi died in May 2017, it was a critical time for the business. We were opening a bunch of stores, and looking to expand our team and our offices. In a lot of ways it was fortuitous that we were so busy, because if we had given ourselves the proper amount of time to grieve, then I don't know how we would have moved forward. As a team, we had tunnel vision. There was too much happening with the business. He was one of my best friends, and I didn't want to let him down.

2. **Was Shashi involved in the business while he was fighting cancer?**

When he got sick, eight months prior to his death, he immediately went into treatment. It was two days later that he stopped coming into the office. All of a sudden, I was running the business alone. His departure affected me so deeply, but we'd been going through a hiring spree, so there were many employees who had little to no emotional connection to Shashi. They knew his story, but they weren't part of it.

3. **While Shashi was alive, did you work through what a transition plan might look like if he didn't survive?**

He had so many resiliencies through his fight. I have text chains up until May 21, the day before his death, about his thoughts on employee benefits that we were pulling together for the team. I think, though, he had resigned himself to the fact that he wasn't going to make it. But I wasn't brave enough to ask him questions about the transition while he was still alive. I ask myself now, Why didn't we talk about it? Instead, I remained optimistic, saying, "You are going to get through this, and you will be at all our new store openings." We all wanted to remain positive for him.

4. **In terms of the business, what was on your mind when Shashi passed?**

Shortly after he died, there was a class action suit brought against us. The plaintiff had purchased products at Credo from three brands we stocked, which stated they were 100 percent natural. The plaintiff argued that they weren't truly natural as they were processed at a manufacturing plant. It is unusual that plaintiffs sue a retailer to get to the brands, but she did, and we had to deal with the case. I thought to myself, Are you kidding me? On top of all of this loss, we have to deal with this case right now? We also had to deal with the optics of Shashi's loss. Our competitors and other retailers were speculating that we would go under. That fueled our resolve. There was no way this was going to break us. Shashi would always say to us, "I think we are on to something big." His words carried me through that time. I just kept my head down and kept thinking, We are on to something big.

5.   How else did his death affect your team?

When Shashi died, we became an instant family. It's one thing to say that you work for a start-up and that you have equity; it's another thing to have your team say, "This is my business too." It was a turning point for us, in which the team took complete ownership over the success of the entire business.

6.   Did any members of the team lose their passion for the business?

We have a store manager, Ally, who started with us from the very beginning. She is like one of my kids, and she had a moment that nearly crushed me. Ally was telling me that the company wasn't the same without Shashi. It had become too corporate. She felt like she didn't know anyone anymore. But during a walk through SoHo in New York, Ally picked up a charm from a store and the word "Shashi" was imprinted on the metal. She saw that and told me she knew everything was going to be okay. He was watching over us.

7.   Describe what the last two years have been like for you personally.

The year 2017 was a really bad year for me; 2018 was even worse. We had to fix many things operationally—from our store build-out process to how we merchandised product. It was like changing the foundation of a house: it's really expensive, and nobody on the outside can see the work it took to fix it. Finally, in 2019, a new dawn emerged, and we have resumed our growth plans. We are opening more stores and hiring more people. We feel good again. During transition periods, you often get distracted by other soul-destroying activities, such as worrying about what the competition is doing or what your competitors are posting on Instagram. I am so grateful to be back to focusing on us and the growth of our business again.

8. **How did you get yourself back to a positive mind-set after a challenging few years?**

Life is about perseverance. We watch our brands go through this too. Many businesses either run out of cash or just get tired. Recently we had a brand, Vapour Organic Beauty, tell us that right before we called them to see whether we could stock them in our stores, they were literally discussing [folding up] their business. They felt like they were working with all of these organic ingredients, but no one cared about the work they were doing. Credo believed in them, and we picked them up for our stores—and now Ancora Partners just invested in them. This is what keeps us motivated. The perseverance of our brands and partners who refused to get knocked down is what got me and Shashi to start this business, and it's what will keep us going. Success was never only about money in the bank. Success for us is about all of the brands that we make successful. They are waiting for us to grow so that they can grow.

9. **What did you learn about yourself through this transformational experience?**

I had no time to prepare before I took over as CEO. Compared to Shashi, I wasn't good at anticipating what was coming next or what the reaction might be at investor meetings. I was grieving, and although our investors were understanding, we still needed to move forward with the business. The problem was, there is a fine line between appearing confident and showing vulnerability. I didn't want my investors to lose faith in me, so instead of asking them for help, I projected faux confidence. They may have mistaken me as not being receptive to their ideas or that I was stand-offish, so it was difficult to build trust with them.

What I did instead was go to all my friends who were in retail and in similar businesses, and I relied on them. And they dropped everything to help me. As an entrepreneur, you can't be afraid to ask for help. Thanks to my support circle, I was able to give our investors everything they asked for in those meetings, but I should have also felt comfortable in myself to ask for help.

10. You hired a new CEO last year; how has she kept Shashi's story alive?

The Investors didn't really sign up for me to run the company. I am an operator. Shashi was the visionary. Last year, I was able to catch my breath and realized we needed a CEO. Being CEO is not what makes me happy. I like opening stores. I like being *in* the stores. We hired a new CEO, Dawn Dobras, and she has been great. We didn't want someone with a huge ego, a huge salary, and an executive assistant in tow. We had a lot of conversations before we hired her, and now she is doing an incredible job. She pays homage to Shashi. She talks about our roots and his story. She is so deferential to him and refers to him all of the time.

Six

Building Team Resilience

A lot of what I want you to learn from this book is how to build resilience as an individual. You'll be hearing "no" a lot, need to make unexpected pivots, and have loads of setbacks. Resilience is one of the character traits an entrepreneur needs the most, and it often takes time to develop. An even larger feat, though, is building an entire organization that is collectively resilient—one that is constantly evolving by anticipating and reacting to change. Changing priorities, heavy workloads, angry clients, staff turnover, supply-chain breakdowns, collaboration with people in different time zones, and missed sales opportunities are some of the common stressors companies face. When these organizational stressors combine with those pounding you from the outside world (such as changing competitive landscapes, industry shifts, economic swings, and technology disruptions), they are bound to take a major toll on a team's ability to bounce back.

The link between a resilient culture and tolerance for risk—meaning cultures that have developed tools to handle the unknown can rebound better than those that haven't—is well documented. For example, a 2015 study of pioneering brands Kodak (maker of camera-related products) and Xerox (known for photographic equipment and paper, i.e., the copy machine) shows why only one of these iconic companies survived in the face of changing competitive landscapes, technologies, and customer expectations.[1] The study deemed Kodak was less resilient with respect to Xerox, because the photography company shunned risk and thereby dramatically lagged behind its competitors. The Xerox team, meanwhile, displayed an appetite for risk and consistently turned internal and external pressures into positive business opportunities.

When you look at other resilient organizations, you discover that they share a common set of traits that help them manage and mitigate risks.

First, resilient businesses have a strong mission and a clearly defined purpose. A good mission statement indicates exactly what, how, and for whom your organization is doing its work. An even better mission statement describes *the value* that is being created for your customer. A purpose-built mission—one that is seamlessly woven into the work a team does on a daily basis—is a powerful motivator and can help your team rebound from failure. The purpose-built mission is the company's reason for being; it is the true soul of any organization.

The second commonality among resilient organizations is the ability to jumpstart productivity. A smart management team questions whether certain meetings or activities are a good use of an individual's

---

[1.]   R. Cuthbertson, P. I. Furseth, and S. J. Ezell, "Kodak and Xerox: How High Risk Aversion Kills Companies," in *Innovating in a Service-Driven Economy* (London: Palgrave Macmillan, 2015).

time. Another thing that can help make employees more productive is adopting techniques such as knocking off the most important thing on a to-do list first thing in the morning, or making a laundry list of bothersome items in order to get them off one's mind. These tactics, when used pervasively throughout the organization, train people to focus and help keep anxiety in check.

The third commonality is having a team that is trained on mindfulness and also given tools to help them handle stress. Individuals who view challenges as within their control do better than individuals who do not.[2] You want your team to be the type of people who believe they have control of the good and the bad that happens in their lives, rather than believing outside forces control their destiny. A company with a collective mind-set that embraces the former view can become unstoppable. When faced with a challenge, a team like this can rely on instinct, planning, and situational understanding to forge a path forward.

Of course, it would be great if we all had the gift of foresight and could plan ahead for every potential outcome, but since we can't, resilience is the next-best skill. It's less about predicting the future and more about having the flexibility to react to and nimbly adapt to challenges. Risk-taking is a great way to practice (and build) resilience, and some companies are even working that idea into their corporate culture. For example, each month, Tata Group (an Indian conglomerate that owns many companies including Jaguar and Land Rover) gives out a "Dare to Risk" award to the employee who has taken the most daring risk during that particular period of time. By doing so, Tata has memorialized risk-taking as one of its key core values.

Resilience is a trait I have tested for in my new-hire interviews for years. Using guidelines from researchers Angela Duckworth and Carol Dweck, I ask a series of questions probing for grit, growth

---

[2.] Kimberly A. Aikens, MD, MBA; John Astin, PhD; Kenneth R. Pelletier, PhD, MD (hc); Kristin Levanovich, MS; Catherine M. Baase, MD; Yeo Yung Park, PhD; and Catherine M. Bodnar, MD, MPH, "Mindfulness Goes to Work: Impact of an Online Workplace Intervention," *Journal of Occupational and Environmental Medicine* (July 2014).

mind-set, and past examples that show a candidate's ability to over-come adversity (e.g., "Tell me about a time when you gave up."). Test-ing for resilience is not foolproof, and even if a candidate displays the ability to bounce back in prior situations, it doesn't necessarily mean those characteristics will be displayed when he or she joins your team. But if leaders don't proactively cultivate their teams to be resilient, stress—from internal or external pressures, or both—can add up. And once it begins to build, a toxic culture can emerge. As a result, people will mismanage their problems, give up, or check out.

How can you avoid the danger that comes from ignoring built-up, unaddressed stress? Here are five ways to keep your team moving forward:

1. First, remind your team of the impact their work has on your customers. Case studies showing your company's im-pact are often seen in sales decks, but are rarely discussed and celebrated as a team. Bring in your clients for a panel discussion, share client satisfaction emails, and conduct a quarterly satisfaction survey to remind people their work matters and is making a meaningful impact.

2. Second, create strong support structures within your team and across departments. Hire a head of talent who can serve as a sounding board. Provide ways in which team members can give encouraging feedback, and discuss that we are all "works in progress," constantly striving to improve. Encouragement goes a long way. Valuing change and professional and personal growth goes even further.

3. Third, encourage your team to recharge their bodies and spirits. Leaders should set examples by working out daily, meditating, or pursuing interesting hobbies. Consider bringing in mindfulness coaches to train teams on letting

go of past hang-ups or future mistakes. It's typically not stress that causes people to give up on their goals; it's the incessant reflection on the past that causes them to throw in the towel. Training the mind to stop the useless chatter allows an individual to move forward.

4. Fourth, provide your team with mentors. Mentors don't need to always come from within your organization. Connecting key leaders with mentors from your personal network can be valuable. Role models can also be found in books and articles. Highlight stories and share them throughout the organization.

5. Lastly, provide latitude. A person's resiliency is strengthened when she feels in control of her own destiny. Teams that make autonomous decisions and reflect on their wins and misses get stronger on their own.

Inside Story
Interview with Nat Turner, Chief Executive Officer and Cofounder of Flatiron Health

Flatiron Health is a healthcare technology company focused on accelerating cancer research and improving patient care. In 2018, Flatiron was acquired by Roche, a pharmaceutical and diagnostics company, for $1.9 billion. Nat Turner oversees all initiatives across provider solutions, clinical oncology, business development, sales operations, legal, and other corporate functions. Before cofounding Flatiron Health, Nat was cofounder and CEO of Invite Media, an advertising technology company based in NYC. Invite Media built the industry's first enterprise advertising platform for buying and optimizing online media in real time. Invite Media was acquired by Google in 2010.

1. **What is your company's mission?**

At Flatiron Health, we want to learn from every cancer patient and improve lives. Today only 4 percent of cancer patients go on to a clinical trial. Of the 96 percent of those who don't enter trials, their medical records are captured but they sit in a storage facility, and the data collected is unused. At Flatiron we aggregate that unused patient data and make sense of it. We then provide it back to the patients, the FDA, pharmaceutical companies, and hospitals to change the way cancer is understood and treated.

2. **Before Flatiron was acquired, it competed against big incumbents who have very deep pockets. How did you teach resilience within your organization in the early days to fight against the competition?**

It is not the easiest to teach resiliency. It is always difficult to get your team to have the same sense of urgency about getting things done, especially when the team has tried a couple of times to solve a problem. One thing we don't do is we don't set artificial deadlines, because they are demoralizing and don't really engender trust. To get people excited, we provide context about what is going on in the market and say, "Here is what competitors are up to." Or we say, "This is what people are saying about us." Zach and I share our opinions and have lunches with the teams. We bring other members of the team, such as our head of sales or our chief medical officer, to present to the board and share the successes and setbacks. Our performance management system is not focused on failure. We care more about how you did something, the things you tried, and what you learned from them to make you and the team better.

3. As second-time entrepreneurs, you've already experienced a lot of the issues that first-time founders face. Did you and Zach experience any obstacles that you hadn't seen in your first business?

In the early days of Flatiron, we got a ton of pushback. My co-founder, Zach, and I did not come from the health-care world. We came from ad tech. We just happened to be very passionate about cancer. We were also in our midtwenties, so we encountered a lot of ageism. The doctors and health-care administrators we were pitching were in their fifties and sixties. We looked like kids. They didn't want to take our meetings, and when they did, they didn't seem interested or trust us. We also didn't talk the talk. We were passionate about cancer but didn't know there were two hundred types of cancer. We didn't know all the terms or the acronyms. Cancer has so many acronyms. The cancer industry is complicated, and it's really its own industry within health care. So we had to learn it all from the ground up.

4. When you were getting rejected how did you feel?

The first twenty or so pitches were really tough. We were pitching a free tool that hospitals could use to receive analytics on their own data—for example, we can help hospitals identify the right patients for specific clinical trials across fifteen different types of cancers based on the data we've aggregated. To us it was a no-brainer, but hospitals were scared of what we were offering. The health-care industry doesn't like taking risks, especially with a little start-up. But for me and Zach, there was really no turning on back. This was our third company, and we were used to taking the punches. There was not a single time that we wished we were working on something else or thought we should give up. It was about reorienting the feedback we were getting. What is the famous quote—Money can't buy you love, happiness, or product market fit? Our product was not resonating with our customers, and we knew we needed to fix the fit in order to be successful. We didn't read the rejection any other way.

5. **Do you feel that your mental agility is greater than most people's?**

My mental agility is high—it has to be when you're an entrepreneur. You kind of have to be crazy to start a company. We decided we were going to build Flatiron, and once we decided, then the onus was on us to figure it out. It might take longer than we anticipated, but once we raised money we felt a deep level of accountability to our investors. If we were bootstrapping the business, we may have wanted to call it quits, but we had 100 percent confidence that we were going to figure out how to be successful. We are all-in kind of guys. There is no half-assing a start-up.

6. **Can you share some of the techniques that you use to work through your hardest problems?**

I have never been a highly spiritual person. I am actually pretty insular. I don't have a life coach. When I'm in the darkest of depths, I usually sit by myself in an unlit room for three to four hours and think through problems. I also find that during my breaks or down time, I have moments of clarity. I like to work through problems on my own. I suppose I'm in a meditative trance when working through problems. It's not a traditional meditation, as the music is blasting and I'm in the dark. I don't get any benefit from sitting and talking about my feelings to other people. I have to work through it on my own and peel away to get to the answer.

7. **Do you try and screen for mental agility in your employees during the interview process?**

I always ask two questions. First, "Explain a tough situation, and how did you react?" The second question I ask is, "What are your two to three biggest failures?" I am looking for candidates who are wired a certain way. Either you are wired for resilience or you are not. As the saying goes, "Everyone has a plan until they get punched in the mouth." Things rarely go according to plan. I like employees who can keep moving despite setbacks.

8. **What are the values that you promote within your culture?**

Across the board, we find that the two values needed to make us successful are, first, being kind and respectful, and being willing to sit on the floor. This can be translated literally and figuratively. There are going to be a lot of smart people in the room, and even if you are senior, you need to be willing to be wrong or not have all the answers. The second value is intellectual honesty. We find that people who are honest and back their ideas up with data are successful. Bezos says it best: "In God we trust. Everyone else bring data."

9. **How do you encourage your team to recharge?**

I was really bad at this until I had kids. I didn't set the right example for the company in our early days. But over time, working until midnight every night is not scalable. Today every team has a budget to celebrate product wins or product releases. We do a better job celebrating our wins and promoting balance. We also stop and reflect on what went well and what we need to improve on future projects. We find that downtime and time to reflect is the best way to recharge.

10. **You've been building your business for close to ten years. What do you do to remain focused on the business?**

I read a lot. While our competitors are going to conferences and moving slow, I am reading. I am strategizing about the future. At the end of the day, resiliency is about having confidence. Some people might think you have some screws loose, but you have to psych yourself up every day. You have to visualize all the successful shots you are going to make. That's the only way to win.

Seven

Foundational Issues: There Is No Such Thing as a Shortcut

When I first launched my business, I had constraints across multiple fronts: time, talent, and money. Because of the constraints I had to take shortcuts. For instance, we used a popular language (PHP) because it's fast and easy to deploy, and it's widely known by programmers. But in the long-term, our tech stack (back-end and front-end technologies) hit limitations. My issue may have been unique to a tech company, but no matter the type of product or service you're launching, you'll end up having to manage constraints. Sometimes you won't be able to use the best ingredients, find the best talent, leverage the most efficient factories, or offer the best amenities. Welcome to start-up life.

Many entrepreneurs believe that you can always retroactively improve your product or service after it's launched. That's not the best way to think. If you take this approach, your business will become strained as it begins to experience user growth. For example, it may become harder and harder to add more users to your platform without slowing down the speed of your product, or the limitations of your tech stack may even threaten a complete crash of the system. Things start to break, your product or service falters, employees feel that working with your product is a hassle, and your customers start complaining. Herein lies the conundrum that most entrepreneurs face at least once (but more likely several times) during their business life cycle: How do you decide when to slow down in order to speed up?

In our early days of JOOR, we didn't have a big enough team to simultaneously work on revamping the product (i.e., changing the programming language we used to code our platform) while continuing to add new features to the existing product. So the question became, Do we jerry-rig our existing product for a little longer and hope it doesn't break at the seams, or do we stop product development and fix things? The first option might miff existing customers, and the second might have precluded us from acquiring new customers.

I needed to figure out how we could navigate these choices and prevail. I felt like I had to trade off either time, quality, or dollars. It was a daunting choice—and one that made me feel like my business could implode at any time. And I've had to make this decision more than once! Re-architecting an entire back-end infrastructure can be a Herculean effort, so oftentimes our team was split on the decision— some advocated for the change, while others wanted to trudge forward hoping not to miss possible revenue opportunities.

What did I do? Well, before beginning a substantial and risky undertaking, I learned to "cleanse" my thinking. This is when I erase any and all feelings that I am a victim of my circumstances. It's so easy to look back and wish you'd made the "right" choices, consulted this person or that one, or pursued a different path altogether. Instead, I remind myself that life is not unfair, and the changes that we need to make will not sabotage the business. Instead, I shift my thinking to the notion that the challenge is here to serve us—to help us get better organized as a team and a business. Flipping this story to one that is empowering gets me energized and excited to move forward.

When undertaking massive foundational changes to your business—whether you're pivoting your revenue model or re-architecting your software platform—you need a significant amount of mental stamina. Many times the task at hand will take several months or even years to successfully complete. At various points during the project, you may find that your efforts are not working and feel an overwhelming desire to abort your mission. To deal with these feelings, I've learned it's best to stop working on the project and give my mind a moment to recover. Stopping doesn't mean taking a week—or even a day—off. It means taking a break for an hour (or less). A few minutes of "zoning out," looking out the window, or going for a walk (without your phone) can go a long way to getting you back on track. Once you've had a chance to get your mind off the issue, come back to it fresh and begin your work again.

Visualization has been a powerful tool for me over the years. I do it with the goal of rewiring my brain to optimize it for success even in the face of severe constraints. The first thing I do is visualize every step in the work plan. I work through everyone's role on the project and each of their tasks from start to finish. Then, I visualize all teams working together in tandem on the project execution. Next, I visualize our clients' interactions with our final work product. I work through three or four scenarios (sometimes more), and try to uncover as many potential roadblocks as I can. Then I visualize the whole process again and again until, in my mind, the project runs without a hitch. I keep visualizing the successful process, and it usually manifests closely to the process I had rehearsed.

Then, with the team, I mentally rehearse or visualize what it will be like to successfully complete the project. We spend a fair amount of team time doing this. We imagine what it feels like to work on the new project. What does is it feel like to re-architect a site? Why is it motivating? Why will we all feel excited once it is done? Visualizing success with your team is worth taking time to do, as it gets everyone pumped to take on the project.

When I have to plan out a big project, another thing I find really helpful is breaking down complex intellectual tasks into smaller ones so that I don't get overwhelmed. When you solve one aspect of a problem, it's much easier to move on to the next issue. Smaller tasks are also better because you can focus intensely on a distinct problem. Once these tasks are outlined, creating a positive mental loop for each of these smaller tasks is valuable. These feedback loops do not always mean celebrating each and every small win. Rather it means acknowledging the benefits from completing the task itself. For example, after completing a task, measure how your work feels—is it getting easier, or are you getting rewarding insights, or are you getting stronger as a business? Find the silver lining in the work you are doing. Hopefully, you will feel a little less overwhelmed than you were a week ago, or even a day ago, and that can go a long way toward strengthening your mental endurance.

Many people I know find the Pomodoro Technique to be powerful for improving mental concentration. The technique calls for breaking up your work in twenty-five-minute increments and then taking a short break before you begin your next task. I find the Pomodoro Technique extremely effective for tasks that I feel less motivated to attempt, such as writing cold-sales emails or doing basic administrative tasks.

When working with teams, it's important to acknowledge and be grateful for your wins. Using celebrations to mark project milestones can be powerful motivators and do wonders for a team's mental stamina. (I personally need to do a better job incorporating this into my work style.) Whether you host a happy hour at work, take your team on an outing, or work out together, it's going to help build camaraderie and give an air of fun to a project that is challenging or daunting. I find stopping to celebrate small wins to be similar to the last resting pose in a yoga practice—Shavasana. Considered the most important pose in yoga, Shavasana requires that a person lie flat on his or her back in corpse pose. Many yogis believe that when you surrender to stillness in Shavasana, you reprogram your central nervous system, allowing for all the benefits of your practice to be absorbed. It's a pose that allows the mind and body to be reborn, and shouldn't be missed. That's how I now think about celebrating quick wins—it helps reprogram me and the team to achieve success.

Anticipating every potential roadblock when you're undergoing massive company change is not possible. There will always be new variables popping up unexpectedly. Things will go wrong. When we re-architected our platform, there were countless times when our website went down or key integrations stopped working. The important thing is to make sure you have a plan for how to deal with these pitfalls and that you maximize the learning opportunities. There will always be a similar project down the road for which your prior learnings will apply.

Inside Story
Interview with Ben McKean, Founder of Hungry Root

Ben is the founder and CEO of Hungryroot, a direct-to-consumer brand of fresh, healthy packaged foods. Hungryroot offers a variety of products, ranging from plant-based pastas and clean-ingredient sauces to delicious proteins and wholesome desserts. From Ben, we learn how his company came back after having to overhaul its supply chain from start to finish.

1. **Can you describe a major project that you undertook in your business that required a lot of thought about whether you should do it or not?**

In 2017, we made the difficult decision to pivot our entire supply chain, transitioning from manufacturing all of our food products in-house to third-party suppliers. This required shutting our business down for six months, foregoing $1 million a month in sales, and closing our two food-production facilities.

2. **How did you weigh the pros and cons?**

Leading up to our decision to pivot, the business had been growing quickly, and we began to recognize that our current supply chain was not set up to scale. We recognized this about six months before we had to make a decision. As a result, the decision was made over a series of conversations between the team and our investors. The risk of making the change was the unknown of a whole new strategy, whereas the risk of continuing to manufacture our products in-house was that we knew it was inherently unscalable. In some respects, we had a lot of time (several months) to weigh the pros and cons, but in January 2017, we had outgrown our in-house production capabilities, and as a result, needed to make a decision very quickly. At that point, it really came down to choosing what we saw as the better long-term path, despite some short-term risks, over the inherently limited path we were on.

3. **How did you mentally prepare for this big change?**

I knew from a logical and rational perspective that it was the right decision for the business, but I needed to prepare myself for the emotional impact the decision would have on the team, our investors, our customers, and myself. In order to prepare for this, I had to remind myself daily that, whatever was going to happen, we had done our best to make the right decision for the company. I did some soul-searching and came to the conclusion that I really did believe that to be true.

4. **Once you were prepared, how did you prepare the team for the change?**

I took a step back from the detail of the decision to talk about the bigger picture, starting with, Why does Hungryroot even matter? We reaffirmed our mission, which is to make it as easy as possible to eat healthy, and we discussed how we needed to offer many different types of food products to customers in order to fulfill that mission. To have product variety, we needed to partner with specialized food manufacturers rather than try to make everything ourselves. As soon as the decision was framed in the context of our mission statement and what is best for the customer, it was easier for the team to understand how and why we arrived at the decision.

5. **Throughout the project, did you experience any road-blocks?**

We experienced so many roadblocks. The biggest challenge was that a couple of people left the company due to the changes we were making. I think most people understood the decision and ultimately agreed with it, but whenever you go through a fundamental change to the business, it naturally gets people to rethink their position in the company and reevaluate their personal goals. It was really tough to have a couple of people leave the company, but always returning to the big picture is what got the rest of us through it.

6. **Did you adopt anything to cope with all of the stress you were experiencing?**

For me personally, I began meditating regularly, as I found it helped me to step back from the stress of the day-to-day and see the larger mission at hand.

7. **What did you do to help your team stay motivated and focused?**

The most important thing was that I stayed focused on, and remained confident in, the big picture. But it was also important that I got my hands dirty and did everything possible to drive progress with the team—from getting on vendor calls to designing the product. We were all in it together, and I needed to reaffirm that daily. Finally, celebrating the small wins was critical. Previously, our sales growth had rallied the team. Now it needed to be milestones like signing on a new supplier or designing our new email sequence.

8. **Was the project ultimately a success?**

Yes! Within six months of relaunching the business in the fall of 2017, we hit $3 million a month in sales, which was three times our previous revenue. Ultimately, customer satisfaction and retention rates were our measurement of success.

9. **What recommendations would you have for an entrepreneur who has to pivot or overhaul his or her product in a major way?**

One of my investors, Jeremy Liew, from Lightspeed Venture Partners, gave me advice that has really stuck with me: he said we shouldn't feel for too long like we are just pushing a rock up a hill. What this means to me is that, while business is hard, it shouldn't *always* be hard. You need to always be searching for ways to make it easier. When the same thing has been hard in the same way for some time, it's a signal that you need to make a change—don't just keep doing the same thing if it's not working. I think that advice really served us well in the decision to explore alternative paths and fix our supply chain to serve us better in the long run.

EIGHT

CAN'T SLEEP AT NIGHT? MAYBE IT'S THE COMPETITION

When I launched my business in 2010, we were a "first mover" in the fashion industry—the only company out there to offer software to brands and retailers that allowed them to buy and sell online. (I'm not talking online shopping for consumers. This was purely a B-to-B operation.) Prior to the introduction of JOOR, retailers would go to trade shows to see a brand's upcoming collection, place a wholesale order in person or after the tradeshow, then receive a paper copy of their invoice. Often the receipts were handwritten.

JOOR is a platform in which brands and retailers can browse through catalogs, place orders, and receive electronic order confirmations online. Ten years ago, believe it or not, this was cutting-edge technology for the fashion industry. Because the ordering process is complicated and requires back and forth communication before the order is confirmed, we immediately attracted a lot of clients and garnered a sizable lead. We knew that should another player enter our market, we had at least a one- to two-year head start.

In an industry that is large and lucrative, competitors will always emerge. If you've already primed the market for your product or service, they will want to capitalize on your success. The market is educated on the need for a product or service like yours, so it is only natural for the customer to want choices. New entrants will convince customers that they can offer a better product or service at a better value.

As expected, one year after we launched, we got wind of a new competitor in the space. By year two, four or five players popped up. Our competitors challenged us on everything from our product design and new features to pricing plans. They talked to our clients, asking detailed questions regarding our product misses, and took full advantage of these opportunities in their pitches. They undercut us on pricing to gain market share, and some even trash-talked us in the market. Others played dirty (like saying we didn't have certain features when we did have them), and they all played hard.

Competitive situations can become all-consuming. We had one competitor who would repeatedly target our entire client list by spreading lies about what our software could or couldn't do. We knew in our heart of hearts that the best way to combat their efforts was to double down on offering our exceptional service. Bad customer experiences are what causes customers to switch. While there is no way we could stop our competition from targeting our customers, we combatted their efforts by cultivating deep customer loyalty.

The team would often get calls from clients accusing us of not having this or that product feature—features that ultimately added

little value to the client—but the competition had riled them up.
As a result, the product team began to have second thoughts about
the product roadmap, and the sales team began to highlight one-off
features rather than discuss how the software as a whole could fit the
client's needs. For me it was mentally draining and caused countless sleepless nights because we were focused on the competition
instead of us as a business. It is really hard to avoid taking things
personally and worrying that you aren't making the right choices. It's
even harder to make sure that your team does not get demoralized
and feel as if they aren't doing enough to stave off competition in
their daily work. To the extent competition becomes a distraction,
it is your job as a leader to shift your mind-set as well as the team's.
Encourage your team to focus on the long-term plan and the things
that will keep clients happy, satisfied, and well serviced.

When the onslaught of competition hits, chances are you'll try
to combat it in one of two ways: emotionally or analytically. It is
easy to go down the rabbit hole of obsessing over everything the
competition is doing: What features are they building? How quickly
are they expanding? What are they hiring people to do?

After our first, most vehement competitor entered the industry,
I put a cross-functional team together. The team consisted of product, sales, customer success, and marketing folks who would stay on
top of what our competition was doing. I thought this would help
us stay on top or predict our competitor's next move. Did it give
us an edge? Not really. All it really accomplished was to make the
team anxious and run me ragged trying to process the information.
Rather than proactively driving the market (that we created), we had
entered a virtual chess game with our main competitor. We'd make a
move, wait for their countermove, then respond with our next move.
Sometimes they acted first, and we'd be put on the defensive. We
moved to a call-and-response mode. We were losing our edge. For a
while, it was fun to rally the team around how slimy our competition
was or how low they would stoop to win business. But in the end,

our task force's work ended up being a giant distraction. We were chasing our tails building features that didn't really serve our clients universally, and spending money on gimmicky marketing materials that produced little return on investment.

Paranoia can be useful but only to a point. After that, it begins to have diminishing returns. Still, it's important to be aware of your competition and their go-to market approach. Learn as much as you can so that your client-facing teams can be smart about what your business can and cannot offer. Educate yourself about your competition's approach and what makes them distinctive. Internalize the findings, but then move back to your vision, executing your strategy and measuring the effectiveness of your tactics. When your team is talking more about the competition and less about the long-term vision, that's when you know you've crossed over to the wrong track.

In any business situation, it's easy to fall into the comparison trap. In fact, I'm sure you've done the same thing in your personal life as well. How do you stop feeling victimized and take your power back? How do you shift your mind-set so you can stop focusing on what is happening externally to what is happening internally?

After about three months of stressing myself out, I'd had enough. I decided to stop dwelling on the competition. I went back to my original vision and strategy. In business as in life, you cannot be all things to all people, so I focused on what we were good at and doubled down on our efforts. We capitalized on our strengths, which were great product design and superior customer service, and drove that messaging home with all of our current and prospective clients.

In the meantime, we built a competitive "moat" around our business, focusing on the seven to ten things that would be difficult for competitors to replicate—or that it would take several years to copy. In the extreme form, these things could be patents or trademarks that a business carries, but typically your moat should consist of a blend of product, service, and reputation offerings that make up your company's secret sauce. Spend time ensuring that your competitive advantage is difficult to replicate.

As a business owner, one of the most important parts of your job is to define and articulate what makes up your competitive moat. Explain it to your team, your clients, and your shareholders. Then consistently uphold, strengthen, and build upon your customer promise.

Shifting my behavior from a reactive mode to a proactive mode was freeing. I transitioned from being less of a victim to more of a fighter. You want to be a boss whose business values are defined, whose competitive edge is clarified, and who is ready to build upon your company's strengths. When you're overwhelmed by competition, this mind-set gives you your power back and keeps you focusing forward rather than looking over your shoulder.

Inside Story
Interview with Courtney Nichols Gould, Founder and Co-Chief Executive Officer of SmartyPants Vitamins

Back in 2011, Courtney and her husband launched SmartyPants, a new and innovative approach to the multivitamin. The messaging (comprehensive single serving, premium ingredients, and delicious without any junk), branding (SmartyPants Because), and product (the vitamins come in the form of gummies) spoke to the hearts and minds of parents and disrupted the stodgy vitamin industry. Soon after SmartyPants' groundbreaking launch, a slew of competitors entered the market.

I interviewed Courtney to understand what was going on in her head while building her one-hundred-million-dollar vitamin empire. I wanted to know how she keeps an eye on the competition while scaling her business.

1. **When you started SmartyPants Vitamins, I think the only vitamin brands that I had heard of at the time were Centrum, Flintstones, and maybe Shaklee. The market was pretty stale. You really changed the game. What is your vision around SmartyPants?**

We launched SmartyPants to change what people had come to expect from a vitamin. We made an all-in-one serving multifunction supplement that is affordable, uses premium nutrients, and actually tastes good. We started with kids in 2011, and then a year later, parents started to ask us to make a similar product for them. We thought we were simply bringing a quality vitamin to the market. But after we launched, we actually backed into a much bigger problem: almost everyone has a hard time taking vitamins regularly. We realized we could do something about solving that compliance issue. We started with gummies because the experience of taking the vitamins was one of the biggest hurdles to consistent use.

2. **There were a lot of copycats that emerged that had slightly different branding, for example, minimalistic or hip branding, or entered via different channels (such as wholesale or retail), but their product was subpar to yours. How did you educate the market?**

About three years after we launched, competitors started to come onto the scene. We were filling a void in the market and inspired others to get on the bandwagon.

Olly was the first competitor that emerged. They seemed to target the single millennial who is more attracted by packaging and positioning, whereas I think we had established ourselves as a product-led company, innovating by using better forms of nutrients and so [attracting] a more discerning customer, which typically is Mom. The founder of Olly, Eric Ryan, also cofounded Method, the cleaning products brand. He is a good marketer and is great at telling his story. In a sense, the entrance of competition was really good for us. We learned to tell our own story, which is about a high level of trust that comes from our laser-like focus on making the best product possible and considering every single thing that makes something "best."

3. What were some of the tactics the competition used against you?

Eric would text my head of sales anytime Olly would land a client. Literally, he would send us a picture of himself walking out of a retailer, saying, "Look which client we just landed." He thought it was funny. At first my head of sales and I were annoyed by it, then we started sending texts back of the same, then we grew up and stopped caring and moved back to doing what we do best: making superior-quality product.

4. Do you think women and men handle competition differently?

Maybe. I was recently at a luncheon with twenty highly successful female CEOs. We were all asked what is something we do to relax. All the women prefaced their responses with, "This is embarrassing, but I do this . . ." or "I shouldn't say this, but I do . . ." They all displayed guilt when talking about how they relax, rather than owning their power. All of these women were badasses but somehow felt remorse when they were asked a simple question about how they unwind. Men don't think twice about answering a question such as this. Women always feel like they aren't doing enough. Perhaps it has something to do with men being comfortable with being hypercompetitive and women being told they should be collaborative. It's something to be mindful of as women take on more leadership roles in the C-suite.

5. What emotions did you feel when serious competitors started to enter the space?

In the first three or four years, we stayed vigilant and looked at all the competition closely. When Olly launched, I was pissed and got a bit nervous. We also compete against Garden of Life, which has been around for twenty years.

I was a competitive athlete when I was growing up—and I still love a good fight. So that was my first reaction when the competition started to heat up: I'm going to dig deep and fight.

But that, in a lot of ways, is wasted energy. I had to stop looking at competition in an absolute sense. It's really more important to view competitors through the eyes of the customer. We decided we were going to be the best at who we are, get that story across to the customer, and then let the customer decide. We wanted to play our own game. We didn't want to design our company around the competition.

6. How has having serious competition impacted you?

I am grateful for the competition. It transformed me. It forced us to ask ourselves: Why are we doing this? Why are we solving this problem? We aren't doing it to make a shit ton of money. It forced us to define what success means to us as a company. Success for us is having the maximum health impact on as many people as we can. We express that mission every day. That's why we are such a big contributor to Vitamin Angels. Through that program we give products to people who can't afford to pay for vitamins, so that they can be healthier. The CEO of Vitamin Angels uses us as an example to inspire other CEOs in our industry to donate and step up their game.

7.   How was your team affected as the competitive landscape heated up?

When the competition heated up, the team mirrored me and my emotions. We have some really badass salespeople who are also former athletes. They were out for blood just as I was, but then they evolved just as I did.

8.   Are you still in hypercompetitive mode—meaning, are you acutely aware of what the competition is doing at all times?

Eventually I returned inward and focused less externally. Supplements is a multibillion-dollar industry. There will be new entrants all the time. And that is a good sign. It means what we are doing inspires others to step into the ring. It forces us to up our game and offer better and better products. Competition validates the entire industry.

Competition is harder when you are small. It was hard for us in the beginning when we had two little kids at home, a mortgage, and had taken no salary for five years. There was so much more pressure to get things right. Today, we have a data analytics team. So we track competition by seeing who is getting more shelf space, and we can see which direct-to-consumer business-es have the money to buy more advertisements. That shows us which of our competitors are doing well.

I actually advise many of the newer players. We have helped a lot of people who are just starting out. It's helpful to get new ideas, and many of the new supplement companies are doing brilliant things. It's helpful to be inspired by and to inspire others. We want the entire industry to rise.

9. What is your advice to entrepreneurs who are dealing with steep competition today?

My advice for those who are just starting out is define your North Star. Always have your mission in mind, remember why you started, and stay true to your story. Hopefully, you are solving a real problem for a meaningful population. When competition pops up, it's easy to lose sight of why you started and it can knock you off your game. Sometimes you think you need to change direction or "pivot," like investors like to say. Or you feel compelled to chase something the competition is doing. You can easily get distracted, and then you create all sorts of fire drills to react to what the competition is doing. In the past, I've allowed this to happen. But now we keep our heads down and I take my own advice. It's made us unstoppable.

10. Unilever recently bought Olly. Do you think about your own exit strategy?

We knew that Olly and Unilever had been in discussion for some time. A lot of investors and companies came to us during that time. It made us stop and think: Should we sell too? We checked in with ourselves and realized that it's not the right thing for us right now, though we may someday in the future. We have more to accomplish. Selling to a larger player might mean deeper pockets, but deeper pockets doesn't always make you a better company.

...

There is no reason to worry so much about your competition, especially in the early days of a business. If you are playing in a multibillion-dollar market and your company hasn't yet reached $100 million in revenue, you're still such a small player that competition shouldn't matter. There is enough room for your business to scale and for others to do the same.

Rather than worrying about the competition, entrepreneurs need to think more about building their competitive moat. Identify the five to ten levers you can pull now that will give your business a sustainable competitive advantage in the next five to ten years. Identify the five to ten bricks you can lay now, and then focus on what you're creating instead of every move someone else is making.

Many leaders say they are grateful for competition and don't resent it. This makes sense because competitors force you to sharpen your strengths and mitigate your weaknesses. Learn from the competition and then return to your grand vision. When you and your team are clear on your mission and how you want to provide your product or services to the world, your passion and commitment will help you work toward that end goal. The competition becomes less and less relevant, and the change you seek to make in the world becomes the only thing that matters.

NINE

LOSING YOUR JOB: WAIT, I'M THE FOUNDER!

For a long time, most conversations about Elon Musk, Mark Zuckerberg, or Jeff Bezos were about how smart, amazing, and innovative they were as company founders. But cut to 2019 and the talk has shifted to, "Does he know what he's doing?" "Can he fix this?" "Is he of sound mind to be in this role?" That's right, even if you're the founder of a billion-dollar company, you can end up in the hot seat. Ultimately a founder works for his or her shareholders, so even if you're the genius behind the whole operation, you're still not protected from being fired. I know this because I started JOOR in 2009 and left in 2017. After leaving, I overcame a lot of guilt and regret and bounced back to a bigger and better life.

But I'm getting ahead of myself. First, I want to mention an interesting debate that's been taking place in Silicon Valley in recent years. At issue is whether companies fare better by retaining the original founder or by hiring a professional CEO. Historically, four or five years after launching, a professional CEO would be brought on board to scale the business and bring necessary structure to an organization. The need for policies, succession planning, and a founder's desire to return to some semblance of work-life balance made the decision to hire an outsider make sense. However, in the last decade, shorter product-life cycles and easier technology deployment allowed for competitors to catch up quickly, resulting in the need for continuous improvement. Founders primarily drive innovation, creativity, and risk-taking—the secret sauce that propels companies forward. The best VCs realize it is more important than ever to retain the ingenuity and hunger in a start-up culture as a company matures.

In the haste of raising capital, it is easy for a founder to overlook legacy planning. Scenarios that might occur seven or eight years down the road are hard to envision or even anticipate. But it is important that you do some up-front work around contingency planning, and there are ways that you can

Protecting your position at your company is important, but sometimes transitions are inevitable and even necessary. So what do you do next? Stage a comeback, of course. In a 2007 article in the *Harvard Business Review*, Jeffrey Sonnenfeld and Andrew J. Ward laid out a framework for a founder's resurrection. They described a path that many great leaders have followed through the years. The four steps are similar to the arc of a hero's journey: decide how to fight back, recruit others to assist in your battle, take steps to recover heroic status, and have the resolve to rediscover your heroic mission.[3]

[3.] Jeffrey Sonnenfeld and Andrew J. Ward, "Firing Back: How Great Leaders Rebound After Career Disasters," *Harvard Business Review*, January 2007.

This formula doesn't just apply to founders; it applies to anyone who encounters a professional or personal setback. More than that, abiding by this framework aids in your healing process. It is a rubric for how to move beyond your past into something potentially better than before.

Let's break down the steps a bit. The decision as to whether to fight back or step aside gracefully often depends on whether the founder wants to feel heard or not. Many founders have the means and experiences to move on, but if they feel they didn't get their "say" publicly, they may feel like they have to fight back. Some leaders who worry about reputational risk choose to fight their dismissal, either through the media or in the courtroom. Others choose to move on gracefully and lie low while working on improving themselves until things blow over. And then there are others who seek to make amends and root for their company's continued success, watching from the sidelines.

Regardless of what you decide, you will need support to help you move forward. In this second step, you may need to get people on your side to help fight your old company, or to just act as a sounding board so that you can move beyond the past. For me, the best way to heal was to focus on creating value. I feel good when I am adding value for others. I put myself in lots of situations where I could be helpful. I advised and invested in start-ups, joined a couple of boards, started a new business, and taught and coached at my alma mater. Having a good sense of what gives me energy—personal growth and contribution—helped me feel like myself again.

Professional networks also can provide a big boost to how you feel during transitional times. Friends will give you support and comfort as you grieve, but your professional network can play a meaningful role in the way you heal. I found myself reaching out to people I hadn't talked to in five or even ten years. Every single person took my call or met me for coffee. Even people who might have been one or two degrees removed provided raw and unbiased thoughts on how to unearth my path forward.

The third step is to recover your heroic status—i.e., regain the status you had before fate dealt its hand. For the best examples of this, look at people such as Martha Stewart or Michael Milken. Fallen leaders make it back to the top by either showing remorse for their prior actions or going on to start new ventures—and working to make them bigger and better than anything they've done before. The best leaders own up to their mistakes and can easily describe what they learned and how they will avoid the same pitfalls in the future. A study published in *Harvard Business Review* found that leaders who own their mistakes and see them as learning opportunities are 50 percent more successful than those who internalize mistakes and are riddled with guilt and shame.[4]

Treating failure like an outcome rather than a permanent state of being is imperative when you have any type of setback. Getting stuck in the past and replaying the movie reel of what happened over and over again doesn't allow you to move forward. The key in my situation was to start taking as much action as I could. Actions that adhered to my personal mission of transforming how people live and work proved incredibly useful. I learned that I really don't care about having a fancy title, a huge salary, or a team of hundreds of employees. When I started seeking out opportunities that allowed me to do that, my lifeblood began to flow again. I got my mojo back.

The final step of full professional recovery, according to Sonnenfeld and Ward, occurs when you assume a new professional role or launch your next endeavor. It's your rebirth. It's your resurrection. When you're able to illustrate that you can operate at a higher level than in the past, others will realize you are an even more worthy leader than before. I don't particularly like the way this step is described, because it places so much emphasis on getting approval from the outside world. Ultimately, happiness emanates from within when you are in alignment with your values. Seeking external validation is a slippery slope, and, at the end of the day, it will not fulfill you. If

---

4. Elena L. Botelho, BJ Wright, and Kim R. Powell, "When Getting Fired Is Good for Your Career," *Harvard Business Review,* October 2018.

you don't like who you are and how you live your life, it will never matter how others perceive you—because you will never be happy.

The real point that I got out of Sonnenfeld and Ward's article is that, with any setback, professional or personal, you must get over the delusion that you can't do "it" again—whatever that "it" is for you. Failing to try again is the only real failure. My next act is in a completely different industry, but it fulfills my definition of success. For me, success is serving happy customers while I consistently evolve and grow my skill set. When I check the boxes on those two criteria, I am fulfilled.

Inside Story
Interview with Renaud LaPlanche, Cofounder and Chief Executive Officer of Upgrade, and Founder of Lending Club (NYSE: LC)

Renaud pioneered online financial lending over a decade ago, establishing affordable personal loans as mainstream affordable credit for consumers looking for an alternative to high-interest credit cards. Renaud's founding of Lending Club in 2006 and his vision have created an entire industry that has since made tens of billions of dollars of affordable credit available to millions of families in America and around the world.

In May 2016, Renaud resigned from Lending Club following an investigation into whether he had violated the company's policies. One year later, Renaud launched Upgrade. Today, as Upgrade's CEO, Renaud presides over the company's business strategy and oversees its execution, developing and offering transparent and affordable consumer credit products. Renaud discusses how he bounced back and the lessons he learned from his transition experience.

1. Can you describe how you felt when you left Lending Club?

My departure from Lending Club was obviously a very painful and frustrating experience. I felt betrayed by several of the people I trusted the most. At the end of the day I took comfort in the fact that I acted honorably and in the best interest of the team, our customers, and shareholders.

2. What did you do immediately after you left?

I took a long and nice vacation. There is no good time to be pushed out of the company that you founded, but if it has to happen, it'd better happen in the spring or summer! I went hiking in the Swiss Alps with my wife and kids, and visited friends and family in my home country of France. It was a good opportunity to get away from all the drama that the press created around me and Lending Club at the time.

3. What thoughts did you have to move beyond? How did you let go of the past?

I tried to stay positive, and really thought in terms of two alternatives: Do I want to fight back and spend the next two years of my life with lawyers and accountants, dissecting every email that I wrote or received over the previous ten years? Or do I want to take that frustration and turn it into something positive, create something new that could help millions of people and make a positive difference in their lives? I chose the latter.

4. Where did you find the energy and inspiration to build something from scratch again?

I think all the support I got from Lending Club's investors, former and current employees, partners, and mere industry observers was a big source of inspiration to get going again. Then we sat down with a few former Lending Club team members and thought about the chance we had to take a fresh look at the model and create a better and more efficient platform that would deliver more value to customers. Many of Lending Club's largest shareholders, and some of the partners who were the most familiar with what happened at Lending Club (such as Jefferies, an investment bank), were the first investors in the new company that I built, Upgrade.

5.   When did you get the idea for your new company?

The idea behind Upgrade is fairly incremental: it really builds up on ten years of online lending, analyzing what worked and what didn't, not just at Lending Club but in the industry in general. We gathered a considerable amount of feedback from investors, partners, regulators, and customers, and used that as a baseline to design a new platform. Then we enhanced it with our own creative thinking about new product ideas that would be truly helpful to American families. There is way too much credit card debt in America (over $1 trillion now). Upgrade's new products can help families better understand their credit situation, better manage it, and lower the burden and cost of consumer credit for everyone.

6.   Why did you decide to start a new company with a business model so close to your former company?

I felt a deep sense of unfinished business. Lending Club was a very promising company on an upward trajectory, and it could have become a lot more than it was at the time when I left. I had a number of ideas that could give life to new products that I thought could continue to transform the financial services industry.

7. Were you concerned that you wouldn't achieve the same level of success as your first company?

No, I think the entire Upgrade team firmly believes we can achieve greater success at Upgrade. We really have taken advantage of our past experiences to build a better platform and design a better strategy than we did in the past.

8. Do you feel like you have conquered your past and live fully in the present?

On good days I do. But, to be completely honest, there are also bad days where I wish I had fought back and told my side of the story. I wish I could let the public know what truly happened at Lending Club and hold everyone accountable for their actions. I might do it one day. But these bad days generally don't last and I get back to building Upgrade. I funnel any leftover resentment and negative energy into our mission of building better credit products that can help millions of families across the country.

9. What advice can you offer on how to turn negative energy into positive energy?

What probably helped me the most was thinking about the impact we could have on people's lives. It is a mission that is way bigger than me. What we are doing helps families and could impact generations to come. That's a wonderful thing about financial services: When products are designed and delivered the right way, they can truly change people's lives for the better. Getting access to affordable credit can profoundly transform a family's situation.

10. **What advice do you have for founders who leave their
    companies?**

I think the process I went through worked well for me; it might
work for others: getting away from it all for a few months. Going
to a peaceful place surrounded by friends and family can really
help you get over the initial shock, disappointment, and frustration. Then turning negative energy into creative energy was a
great way for me to stay positive and build something new.

TEN

SACRIFICE FOR WHAT?

Countless stories exist about entrepreneurs who sacrifice every-thing to build their businesses—from personal relationships, finances, health, and friends to everything in between. I was one of them. My belief before starting my business was that sacrifice was the only way to build a successful business. After going through it once, I now understand that I don't need to sacrifice everything if I have a proper system in place. Five years into building JOOR, I wouldn't have been able to tell you the last time I'd worked out. I wasn't sleeping or dealing with my personal finances (I'm relieved

I wasn't bouncing checks), or spending more than an hour with my young children each day.

Thankfully, I have a great spouse, a nanny, and supportive parents who shouldered most of the load. But it is safe to say that when my spouse and I were both busy and my parents or nanny weren't around to help, our relationship was strained. I was in a perpetual state of guilt, and my husband often resented me for putting the business in front of everything else.

Sure, anything worth having requires focus and sacrifice. This means that sometimes you may neglect areas of your personal life when you're building your professional life. But does it have to be that way? Why are we conditioned to believe that sacrifice, pain, and single-minded focus is the only way to achieve success in business?

Picking my head up after several years spent building the company was a rude awakening. My health was suffering, and my body was breaking down. I had constant back or neck pain. My eyes were bloodshot all the time from the frequent travel overseas. I couldn't sleep without checking my email multiple times throughout the night. I didn't realize the way in which I was operating until I looked in the mirror one day. I literally couldn't stand up straight or push my shoulder blades together. I was permanently hunched over and in pain.

At this point, I asked myself whether the continued sacrifice was ultimately worth it. The answer was a big fat NO. Entrepreneurship— or any job, for that matter—shouldn't mean the ultimate sacrifice. With planning, organization, and coaching, you don't have to neglect all other aspects of your life. In fact, I believe organizing the rest of your life can set you up for even greater success in your professional life. If I were still at JOOR, I have no idea whether I would have paused to check in on how I was doing in every aspect of my life outside of work. I feel horrible when thinking about the permanent damage that I might have inadvertently created in my life had I stayed.

Within a year after leaving my company, I'm happy to say I got myself back on track. I knew the fastest way to make it happen was to enlist help. I found a coach, role models, or mentors for every aspect of my life. It was so helpful that I thought it made sense to find other motivating people to help me grow in other parts of my life. You don't have to spend a lot of money to do this. Coaches can be informal and take the shape of mentors, friends, or inspiring role models you find through reading biographies or even blogs.

My biggest area of neglect when I was building my business was my finances. We were spending money on wasteful things in the name of convenience, and we weren't investing our savings. The stock market was at an all-time high, and we weren't reaping any of the benefits of a strong market. My husband and I had little strategy to get back on track, so we hired a wealth manager to help us invest our money across real estate, stocks, and bonds. Many people use Betterment or Wealthfront or other online financial advisors, for which they pay a small fee. Thanks to our money manager, we came up with a personalized strategy to diversify, cut unnecessary spending, and create streams of passive income. Regardless of how you allocate your finances, the most important thing is to make a plan that doesn't require daily attention and that you can believe in for the long haul.

As part of this financial makeover, I started tracking my household expenses. What's funny is that when I was running my business, I was watching each and every expense, but I wasn't doing this type of analysis for our personal finances. Using a basic app such as Mint, I started tracking our family's spending. That made it very easy to cut extraneous costs that were a result of overbuying in the name of convenience (the bulk "everythings"—garbage bags, snacks, water, toothpaste, etc.), buying unnecessary items for our children out of guilt for not being present, or making impulse purchases that never got used.

Our next step—which took some forethought and time—was to create additional semi-passive revenue streams. The whole idea behind this is to make additional money "while you're sleeping." We bought a few rental properties and franchises, and launched a direct-to-consumer business. These revenue streams require due diligence, but once you put in the effort up front, you only have to spend a few hours a week or month managing your investments.

My second-biggest area of neglect was my relationships. In talking to one of my mentors, I created a methodology to help strengthen the relationships that mattered to me: immediate family, close family and friends, professional friends, new friends I wanted to make. For each of these relationship categories, I created a list of goals related to the frequency, quality, and types of activities we could do together. I started calling my parents regularly. I hosted a dinner party with different friends once a month and started making new friends again. I feel more connected and happier as a result.

Another area in my life I wanted to refocus on was my health, which I defined as mind and body. I knew working out daily was important, but I also wanted to meditate. Like any newbie, I had trouble sitting still, so I would often give up. I worked with a spiritual guru on this, and she gave me a mantra that I can chant silently instead of forcing my mind to be still. I do this for ten minutes each morning, and if my thoughts deviate, I simply come back to this mantra. (Meditation mantras are highly personal, so I'm not going to share mine, but if you need some inspiration, try using Insight Timer, a free app with thousands of guided meditations and mantras to chant to get you started.) For a physical recharge, I work with a mixed martial arts trainer who helps me keep my weight stable and my muscles strong and defined. These practices take about one hour each day, combined, and because I enlisted friends and coaches, I have reached my goals faster than if I had done it by myself. For me, progress equals happiness, and that motivates me to keep going.

To help bring more joy back into my life, I knew I also needed to tend an area I broadly think of as spirituality. It is important to constantly refill your well; otherwise, burnout is inevitable. For many years, I really had only one focus (work), and I didn't realize I needed inspiration from many different sources to keep innovative ideas flowing. So now, twice a year, I do something unexpected. This could mean taking a trip, attending a conference, or picking up a new hobby. Last year, I fulfilled this goal by learning to box and practice yoga. This year I am learning chess, attending a ten-day silent meditation, and trying heli-skiing.

Having additional family time, spirituality, and workouts in my life has been incredible, but I wouldn't feel like myself if I didn't work. And, ironically, in my post-JOOR epiphany, I realized I had also been neglecting my professional goals. I now am part of a small professional group that helps me stay on plan. We meet once a month and discuss progress against our goals. My goals consist of growing my company revenue, mentoring other entrepreneurs, and funding other start-ups while not compromising on physical, spiritual, and mental well-being.

Looking back, one thing I've learned is that you shouldn't wait until you've achieved that one thing that matters to you the most (building a business, losing weight, meeting your dream partner) to figure out the other areas of your life. If you knew you were going to die in a year, what would you regret not having done? Set goals for each area. I don't make daily ones, because they're too difficult to track, so I set monthly goals in each area, which also tends to take a lot of the pressure off of my day-to-day. Setting goals up front and then leveraging a coach in each area to help me stay on task has been successful. In areas where I don't have a coach, I count on my husband and kids to keep me on track.

While the outcomes for all my goals are measurable, I've found that the biggest hurdle has been deciding that I am committed to them. Just as in business, coming up with a meaningful *why* helped me do this. I used to beat myself up when I didn't stick to something, and I thought that I wasn't mentally strong enough to conquer the goal. It took me a long time to learn that it wasn't an issue of willpower (which I don't even think is a real thing anymore). It turns out I hadn't fully decided I was going to commit.

Let me go back to my yoga practice for a minute. I always liked the idea of being a yogi, but I never had the patience for it. When I couldn't master a certain pose, I would get disenchanted. I'd also miss the sweaty calorie-burn that I got from a long run or another heavy-duty workout. I couldn't find the discipline to keep practicing. Only recently did I realize I simply hadn't fully decided I wanted to put in the effort to learn the poses or make the time for daily practice.

When I finally defined my *why*—that when I practice yoga I remember to breathe, and that gives me control over my mind and actions and helps me stay calm in almost all circumstances—I no longer needed an internal pep talk to psyche myself up to do it. And because I want to hold on to that superpower, I readily keep up my daily practice.

When I think about all of the things I ignored or missed out on while I was so immersed in my company, it makes me feel dispirited. So, speaking from experience, I want to reiterate: you don't need to sacrifice everything as an entrepreneur. In fact, don't do it. You have more of a shot at being successful if your "house" is in order. It will give you the sustenance to give more of yourself to your team, and you will be less distracted by unwanted (and unproductive) emotions. Feelings of guilt, deprivation, and resentment will fade back and make room for inspiration, clarity, and innovation.

Inside Story
Interview with Betty Liu, Founder of Radiate and currently the Executive Vice Chairman for the New York Stock Exchange (NYSE)

Betty founded Radiate in 2016. Radiate provides online content from empowering leaders who offer expert advice. NYSE acquired Radiate in 2018, where it continues to grow through NYSE's platforms. Betty was also an award-winning business journalist who anchored the Bloomberg Television program *Daybreak Asia*, and she co-created and anchored the network's *In the Loop* program for eight years.

1. When you were running Radiate, what were the biggest
    sacrifices you made while running your start-up?

It's hard for me to call things sacrifices, because it was a choice
I made to start my own company. Nobody forced me to do it.
There were some things I knew I'd have to give up or minimize in
order to start a business—chief among them was my personal life.
Other than spending time with my kids, I pretty much curbed a
lot of the socializing I used to do with friends. I just had no time.

2. Besides your social life, can you talk about other areas that
    you neglected that you now realize are important?

Being physical is very important to me because without your
health, you have nothing. I don't always do great in this area, and
during the time I was starting my business, my back gave out
and I had to have back surgery. I still hold it as my number-one
priority, but I didn't always practice what I preached.

Mental and spiritual fitness are also very important. Being an
entrepreneur is a real test of your mental toughness. If you can
persevere through the tough times and not give up, then you'll be a
great entrepreneur. I also think spirituality has helped me through
the toughest moments. An entrepreneur friend of mine told me
that when she was starting her business (and it's very successful
now), she always looked for signs that she was on the right path.
Maybe it was getting that phone call at the critical moment. Those
things are important to keep your momentum and spirits up.

3. Have you evolved your definition of balance?

I don't really have balance, but I do make sure to carve out
personal time and stick to it. I don't think I've ever had balance,

because that sounds like things have to be fifty-fifty. My life has never been 50 [percent] work and 50 [percent] personal. Now I've learned to integrate both, and just made sure to prioritize the two areas when I needed to.

4. **Do you recommend that other entrepreneurs try to achieve some sort of balance in their personal and professional lives?**

There is no question balance is going to be harder to achieve when you become an entrepreneur. Work-life integration becomes a way of life. That's because you'll be constantly thinking about your business, and ideas will pop up all the time, and it will be difficult to turn off your brain during personal time. Therefore, I don't recommend balance so much as being conscious to carve out time for your personal life and stick to it. I did my best thinking about the business on days off when I didn't look at my phone or do any work. That space you carve out is essential to your mental health and will make you a better entrepreneur.

5. **How do you know when you are "in balance"? (e.g., What does it feel like?)**

I think when you are in balance, it's more like you are "in the groove." Things are flowing. Your team is on the same page with you; clients are happy; your family seems happy. Those moments can last for a while or they can be upended by a new development.

6. **In your experience, what is the best state of mind when launching and scaling a business?**

I think you really have to do it for the right reasons. Are you passionate about your company's mission? Would you be willing to do it even if you weren't being paid? Is there really a need for what you're creating? I wouldn't do it if you feel bored, and you shouldn't want to be an entrepreneur because it sounds glamorous, because it really isn't. Everyone has different motivations for wanting to start their own businesses, but I think some of what I mentioned above is critical.

7.   What type of mental preparation do you recommend entrepreneurs use to prepare for the highs and lows of running a business?

I suggest you really get used to the word "no." There will be a lot of people who tell you no. No to funding your business. No to buying your product. No to partnering together. I really think the best entrepreneurs are those who persevere—when they hit a wall, they don't back down but find a number of different ways to get over that wall.

8.   What type of support system did you rely on during your entrepreneurial journey?

I had some great advisors and investors who would answer my calls or grab lunch or dinner anytime to work through problems. They never told me what to do, but always gave me enough advice for me to make the best decision. They also would tell me if I was being pig-headed about something. I always appreciated their honesty. I also have to give some props to my two teenage boys. They did not know what their mother was getting into, but they knew that if things failed, I would be out of a job and maybe would have to sell the house. They didn't flinch, and even started packing things up just in case!

9. **When an entrepreneur has a major setback or experiences failure, how do you advise that she/he get through it?**

It's a big punch in the gut when something you thought was going to work out ends up failing. I don't fault anyone for needing a day to recover—perhaps go home, turn on Netflix, and eat some ice cream to feel better. However, the next day, it's back at it. Don't let that moment define your company or yourself. Three weeks later, you'll have forgotten how bad the setback felt.

10. **What tips can you offer entrepreneurs who don't want to sacrifice "everything" to achieve success?**

I really don't believe you should sacrifice everything to be an entrepreneur, but you do have to be willing to put it all on the line—i.e., your reputation, your money if you need to, your complete 100 percent effort. Entrepreneurs are hustlers, and if you don't like the idea of hustling to make the first sale, get the first investment, or recruit your first team members, then don't do it.

PARTING THOUGHTS

B efore you go, I want to talk a bit more about spirituality. I believe all entrepreneurs are spiritual by default. Whether you're part of the subset that embraces the seven principles discussed in this book or you follow another set of beliefs, in order to survive the crazy, challenge-filled, unexpected world of entrepreneurship, you will have to rely on spirituality in some shape or form.

Here's why: Ever since we were little, we've been conditioned to follow the rules. Color within the lines. Turn in our homework on time. Write an English paper using a particular framework. The structure we've been given is intended to help us succeed. But when we're forging a new path, we have to approach work and life differently—that is, without structure. This new path may seem inconceivable to others, but it's what forces all entrepreneurs to dive deep, sift through the ambiguity, and create a playbook of rules that are all their own.

Finding your flow as an entrepreneur doesn't happen automatically. It takes confidence, time, and tenacity to develop. You'll need to know yourself really well to figure out the structure that will help you to be your best creative self and make progress toward your vision. You'll need to quickly assess your learnings from failures and success, let go of what doesn't work, and keep what does. All of this takes intuition and heightened perception, which only comes with flexing your spiritual muscle. To put it another way, looking inward is by definition the meaning of spirituality.

This book is meant to guide you to the point where all of this makes sense. I recognize that the lessons that will resonate the most with you are those that match up to where you are now in your journey. So I'd encourage you to use this book as a reference—something you can come back to during particular challenges or times that call for strategizing. My hope is that this book will serve as inspiration and comfort, reminding you that you aren't alone. Many entrepreneurs are experiencing (or have experienced) the same things that you are. I hope you find solace here, and I also encourage you to seek out like-minded founders who can support you along the way.

As an entrepreneur, day in and day out you are asked to face your fears, think through tough problems, and continuously rise to the occasion. My belief is that embracing a spiritual approach early in your entrepreneurial journey will help you cope with any obstacles and achieve your dreams faster.

ABOUT THE AUTHOR

Mona Bijoor is a partner at King Circle Capital LLC, an investment firm, where she has holdings in real estate, franchises, start-ups, and online businesses. Mona is also the founder of JOOR, the premier online global B2B marketplace for wholesale buying that directly connects brands and retailers.

Mona's experience as a brand consultant for the fashion industry and within buying departments for global retailers inspired her to create JOOR in 2010 to solve some of the incredible challenges and time constraints she encountered during her career. By 2016, she had grown the company to process over $10 billion in gross merchandise value. Based in New York City, Mona expanded to offices in Los Angeles, London, Paris, Milan, Sydney, and Melbourne, increasing the team to one hundred employees worldwide. Clients include Neiman Marcus, Harrods, Michael Kors, and Kate Spade. While at JOOR, Mona was recognized by Crain's 40 under 40 and Wharton's 40 under 40, as well as receiving the Big Apple Entrepreneur of the Year Award. She is a frequent contributor to *TechCrunch, Entrepreneur,* and *HuffPost.*

Mona earned a BA from the University of Pennsylvania and an MBA from the Wharton School of Business. She currently lives in Brooklyn with her husband and two daughters.

Made in the USA
Middletown, DE
18 January 2020